WHAT TO SAY WHEN YOU TALK TO YOUR SELF

WHAT TO SAY WHEN YOU TALK TO YOUR SELF

Shad Helmstetter, PhD

GALLERY BOOKS

NEW YORK LONDON TORONTO SYDNEY NEW DELHI

G

Gallery Books
An Imprint of Simon & Schuster, Inc.
1230 Avenue of the Americas
New York, NY 10020

Published by arrangement with the author

First Gallery Books trade paperback edition June 2017

Manufactured in the United States of America

20 19 18 17 16 15 14 13 12

Library of Congress Cataloging-in-Publication Data is available.

ISBN 978-1-5011-7199-4

CONTENTS

WHAT TO SAY WHEN YOU TALK TO YOUR SELF

INTRODUCTION

to the Updated Edition

Discoveries in the field of neuroscience that made the first edition of this book possible have expanded—or rather exploded—into every area of our culture. The concept of positive self-talk has grown from a breakthrough in the field of personal growth to a much broader and more enlightened understanding of the brain's role in human behavior and how it works in the lives of every one of us.

Today, most people understand that we get programmed from birth—that our brains are literally wired for success or failure—and that we end up living out those programs, for better or for worse. But many people still struggle to get rid of the old programs that are negative or are holding them back, and aren't sure how to overcome them. Research in neuroscience has shown us how the brain gets programmed, and people want to know how they can use that knowledge to change their programming and improve their lives.

In that quest, this new edition will guide you well. The complete story of self-talk, how we get programmed and what to do about it, is all here, updated, and ready to help.

From time to time I will restate, in different ways, points that are especially important for you to retain. This is based on the rule of neuroplasticity, which has shown that our brains become wired with new information—strongest and fastest—with *repetition*. When you notice any point that is repeated, it's there to help you wire it in, and it's a point you'll want to keep.

Presenting this new edition also gives me the opportunity to thank the many tens of thousands of my readers who have read this book in many languages around the world, and who have made positive self-talk a part of their everyday lives. If what is magic today becomes the science of tomorrow, then what was the "magic of self-talk" just a few years ago has now become the burgeoning science of a whole new way of life.

Shad Helmstetter, PhD
February 2017
www.shadhelmstetter.com

CHAPTER ONE

Looking for a Better Way

You are everything that is,
your thoughts, your life, your dreams come true.
You are everything you choose to be.
You are as unlimited as the endless universe.

Life, for most of us, should be pretty good.

We have all heard what life is *supposed* to offer: endless opportunities, the fulfillment of our dreams, and a chance to live each day in a way that brings happiness and success. Most of us want and need at least a successful job or career, a good family life, and reasonable financial security. We expect that from life. We know deep inside that we deserve our fair share and we have every right to attain it.

Have you ever wondered, then, why things don't work out the way they should? Why do we not get from life many of the things we would like to have—and feel we should? Why do some people seem to be "lucky," while the great majority of the rest of us seem not to be?

Why are some people, day to day, happier, more productive, more fulfilled than others? What makes the difference? Is it kismet, a kind of fate, that in some mysterious way charts our destiny and leaves little of the steering of our course through life up to us?

Is the control of our lives in our hands or isn't it? And if we can, or *should,* control our lives, what goes wrong? What holds us back? If we truly would like to do better, be the way we really would like to be, and be happier and more successful every day in every area of living, *what is the wall that stands in our way?*

AN UNLIMITED LIFE OF PRACTICAL POTENTIAL

Imagine living a life that did not give in to the barriers and the battlements, the hassles and the hurdles of everyday living. Imagine a life filled with the vitality of achievement and the enrichment of daily self-fulfillment. To me, for a long time, that kind of life sounded like an impractical dream, a cardboard box filled up with daydreams and wishes. To live a life of hope, promise, expectation, and achievement was to live the life of someone who lived only in the pages of a book.

When I was quite young, I had a soaring imagination. Long before I learned what we could *not* do, I dreamed of doing what I knew we *could*. I remember, as a young boy, lying on my back in the cool, soft grass late at night, my mind sinking upward into the depths of the crystal-clear stars that blanketed the summer sky above me. I could reach out and touch those stars. I could imagine any dream and see it come true.

It was only later that my dreams gave way to more practical considerations. Star-filled heavens, dew-soaked grass, and princely dreams of imaginary kingdoms bowed to more rational requirements. As I began to pursue my education in earnest, I began to learn what we could *not* do. In time, I became more intent on studying the laws and the limits of man than on learning the far-reaching extremities of mankind's potential.

I learned all of the "shoulds," "musts," and "can*nots*." I was told that it was bad to have your head in the clouds and it was good to have your feet on the ground. So I extracted my head from the magical excitement of the universe and got down to business learning about the more practical matters of survival and acceptance. From time to time I had the nagging suspicion that there was more to all of this than was meeting the eye—I just couldn't see it yet.

It was years before I decided it was time to stop and look at the stars again. But I did. The result of that one small decision changed my direction and my life.

By the time I stopped and sank once again, upward, into the stars, I had completed a twenty-year odyssey that took me from the back roads of a farmland village to the towering offices of New York's Madison Avenue; from a quiet countryside of wheat fields to the negotiating tables of three-piece-suited attorneys and well-groomed marketers. My odyssey took me to snow-covered midwestern college campuses, and to palm-lined streets of western universities.

Somewhere, during that time, I began to wonder and dream again, as I had as a young boy years before. What if we *could*? I wondered. What if we could find what's stopping us and turn it around? What if there *is* an answer and no one else has looked in the right place? What if any of us, at any time, could reach up *and touch the stars*?

I began the first part of my search by studying something called "human behavior." That's something you can get a degree in without ever really figuring it out. It is also something that older people seem to know more about than younger people. No matter how many educational degrees my professors could profess, I suspected that some of the silver-haired older people I knew had figured out what human behavior was all about long before we were taught courses in the subject.

I next studied something called "motivational marketing." That teaches us what makes people do what they do even when they don't want to do it. When I completed my course work, it was my final opinion that you can never really get anyone to do anything they don't want to do unless you use force. I decided that in most of the world, "force" is called "advertising."

In time, I found myself walking the hallways of academic psychology. It is a good field and it deserves our attention and respect. A lot of people have lived richer lives because someone who cared took the time to listen.

Yet despite all the good people I encountered and the useful information I learned along the way, nowhere in my studies of business, religion, motivation, or psychology had I found a concrete solution to the question of how the average individual could touch all the stars in his or her heaven and still keep both feet on solid ground.

Eventually, I recognized that if I was going to find what I was looking for, I would have to set a new course and search in a different direction. To find the specific answer I sought, I would have to embark upon a journey of my own.

I knew there had to be a better way, something that was obvious perhaps, something that might have been overlooked. I believed that mastering one's future must surely start with managing one's "self." And if we could accomplish that, we could manage and master at least a part of what we call "life."

As I continued to study the inner workings of the human mind, I decided to look further into the brain itself. And it was there that, in time, I found many answers—and one simple, undeniable solution that would shed life-changing new light on why we, as humans, fail to live up to so much of our incredible potential . . . and what we can finally do to change that.

CHAPTER TWO

The "Answers"

There is always an answer, of course. There are countless self-help "answers" that any of us can find in any bookstore or seminar classroom. If we are to believe what we read on the dust jackets of self-help best sellers, or hear from dynamic speakers onstage, all any of us has to do is read the right book or attend the right program and, beginning tomorrow, we will be able to change what we would like to change, live better, and find the achievement each of us is seeking.

For many years, I studied the philosophies of success, analyzed the lists of instructions—the "how-to's" of making more money, being a better manager, losing weight, overcoming depression, getting a better job, setting goals, living with others, managing time, or just generally "being more successful." I tried the success techniques for myself and talked to dozens of others from many walks of life who had done the same. I talked at length with many of the leaders of the success industry—corporations whose business it is to teach us to be more successful.

I talked to the customers who attended the seminars, bought the books, or listened to the audio tools and watched the videos. I talked to the employees of the companies who were in the business of helping people become successful, to learn if they, too, applied the principles that their companies promoted. To learn what really "worked," and what did not, I immersed myself in the world of success, examining every facet of that fascinating field from the inside out. I consulted with the leaders of the industry. I examined their methods, their systems, and their solutions.

And in all that time of studying so much of the field of success, I found a consistent promise—the promise of our success, waiting just around the corner.

But as I read the books, studied the seminar concepts, and examined the best of the best motivational tools and techniques available, I realized that promise was, ultimately, unfulfilled.

I saw that even the best-selling success solutions were able to create *lasting* changes in only a handful of the tens of thousands of people who tried them. They would work for a time, and then the average individual would revert to his old ways. After the first excitement of the brand-new self-belief wore off, the dreams soon gave way to the realities of everyday living.

Have you ever attended a function or a meeting in which someone gave a rousing motivational talk? Have you ever read a book that caught your attention as being life changing, gotten excited and motivated to put the ideas into practice, only to have the book wind up forgotten on a dusty bookshelf next to other great ideas like it?

Have you ever been inspired to change, to achieve something important, and then stopped? Where did the inspiration and the motivation go—and why didn't it *last*?

If there are so many answers to our questions about what to do to make life better, why have so many people failed at making these great ideas work? Or if they worked for a time, what makes them stop working?

It became obvious to me after all my research that within the information on how to lead a better life, how to find more happiness and personal fulfillment, *something vital was missing*. It was something so essential, so important to the whole process of achieving success that, without it, the solutions wouldn't work—at least, not for any length of time.

The problem is not with the books. The problem is not with the seminars or with the motivational talks. There are a lot of personal growth concepts and techniques that are wonderful. They *could* work—and they *should*. There has to be a good reason why the help they give us isn't permanent.

After studying the success ideas and solutions that could work *for* us, I began to recognize that there was also something working *against* us.

FINDING A SOLUTION THAT LASTS

I was quite young when I first heard the biblical passage that reads, "As a man thinketh, so is he." I recall shaking my head, thinking that could not be. How could we possibly *be* what we think? After all, isn't our physical self one thing, and our private thought another?

Little did I (or most of us then) understand that the biblical passage had hit the nail of truth squarely on the head. It would be years later, however, after following the discoveries through which modern-day neuroscientists had begun to unlock the secrets of the human mind, that I would come to know just how correct—how *scientifically* correct—that biblical passage had been.

After you examine the philosophies, the theories, and the practiced methods of influencing human behavior, you'll find, as I did, that it gets down to the truth of one powerful fact: You will become what you think about most; *your success or failure in anything, large or small, will depend on your programming—what you accept from others, and what you say when you talk to yourself.*

At the time I first recognized that this one simple clue could lead to a breakthrough in individual attitude and performance, most of what we thought we understood about the human brain was little more than speculation. Medical researchers and neuroscientists had not yet explored or mapped the mazes of the brain to the extent that they have today. Few of the brain's complex electrochemical mysteries were fully understood.

But today, as research continues, the brain is giving up more and more of its secrets. Each day more progress is made, and researchers have learned to anticipate an unending drama of new discoveries.

An understanding of an incredibly important function of our own personal computer—the human brain—is what has been missing from most of our attempts at creating formulas for personal growth.

The answer to the problem turned out to be the result of something that had been almost entirely overlooked: We are trying to force the brain to do something that it has not been programmed to do. We want to create success with "rules of success," but that's not how the brain works; *that's not how the brain is wired.*

The reason why some people accomplish nearly any task more easily than others, achieve their goals more readily, and live their lives more fully, is this: Those who appear to be "luckier" than the rest have actually only gotten better mental programming to begin with, or have learned how to erase their old negative programming and replace it with something better.

In the last few decades, we have learned more about the workings of the human brain than was known throughout all history prior to that time. We now know that by an incredibly complex physiological mechanism, a joint effort of body, brain, and "mind," we become the living result of our own thoughts.

It is no longer a success theory; it is a simple but powerful fact. Neither luck nor desire has the slightest thing to do with it. It makes no difference whether we *believe* it or not. *The brain simply believes what you tell it most.* And what you tell it *about you,* it *will* create. It has no choice.

Through scientific discovery in the field of neuroscience—research into how the brain works to affect every moment of our day-to-day lives—we have proved the relationship between our own programming (how we are mentally "wired") and our success or failure in any endeavor we undertake, from something as important as a lifetime goal to something as small as what we do in a single day.

Have you ever considered just how much of what you do—how you act, how successful you are—is dependent on the conditioning, the programming you received from others, and on the conditioning you subsequently accepted and kept giving *yourself*?

It is virtually impossible for any of us to do anything, no matter how insignificant, without being affected by that programming. Every step you take, move you make, and word you say is affected.

It follows that if every action you take, of any kind, is affected by prior programming, then the end results of your actions are equally affected—in short, how successful you will be at *anything* is inexorably tied directly to the words and beliefs about yourself that you have stored in your subconscious mind.

And what is stored there, for most of us, was decided for us by someone else.

The human brain, that incredibly powerful personal biochemical computer that each of us has, is capable of doing for you anything reasonable that you'd like it to do. But you have to know how to treat it; you have to know how to wire it in the right way. If you do it right, and give it the right directions, it will do the right thing—it will work for you in the right way.

If we give our mental computer the wrong directions, it will act on those wrong directions; it will continue to respond to the negative programming that we and the rest of the world have been giving it. We have literally been wiring our brains in the wrong way, *physically*—without even being aware of it.

THE 148,000 "NO'S"

I'll give you an example of some of the negative programming most of us have received, the kind of programming that, along the way, eventually got hardwired into the physical structure of our mental computers. And those seemingly harmless words build up inside our subconscious minds, word by word and thought by thought, eventually creating a brick wall of failure we often don't see, much less know how to fix. Here's how it works.

During the first eighteen years of our lives, if we grew up in fairly average, reasonably positive homes, we were told "No" or what we could *not* do, or what would not work, more than *148,000 times.* If you were more fortunate, you may have been told "No" only 100,000 times, or 50,000 times—however many, it was considerably more negative programming than any of us needs.

Meanwhile, during the same period, the first eighteen years of your life, how often do you suppose you were told what you *could do* or what you *could* accomplish in life? A few thousand times? A few hundred? During my speaking engagements to audiences across the country, I have had people tell me they could not remember being told what they *could* accomplish in life more than three or four times!

Whatever the number, for most of us the "yes's" we received simply didn't balance out the "no's." The occasional words of "belief" were just that—occasional—and they were far outweighed by our daily doses of "cannots."

This negative programming that we all received (and still receive) has come to us quite unintentionally: It has come to us from our parents, who wanted to protect us; it has come to us from our brothers and sisters, from our teachers, our schoolmates, our associates at work, our lifemates, advertising of all kinds, the six o'clock news on television, and unlimited posts on the Internet.

Leading behavioral researchers have told us that as much as *77 percent* of everything we think is negative, is counterproductive, and works against us. At the same time, researchers have said that as much as 75 percent of all illnesses are self-induced. It's no wonder. What if the researchers are correct? That means that as much as 77 percent or more of our programming is the wrong kind.

Until recently, no one understood well enough the human mind—how the human brain gets wired and rewired—and that this programming and wiring process goes on throughout our entire lives. The result was that without knowing what they were doing, and with us not recognizing the immense effect this "casual" programming was having on us, *without anyone being aware of it,* everything and everyone around us has been programming us.

THE POWER OF REPETITION

Unfortunately, most of the programming we received was the wrong kind of programming—but we took it to heart, and our brains wired it in. Year after year, word by word, our life scripts were etched by others. Layer by layer, nearly indelibly, our self-images were created.

In time, we ourselves joined in. We began to believe that what we were being told by others—and what we were telling ourselves—was true. No matter how innocently given or subtly implied, we began hearing the same words and thoughts repeatedly; hundreds, even thousands of times we were told, or we told ourselves, what we could not do, could not accomplish. *Repetition is a convincing argument.* Eventually we believed what others told us and what we told ourselves most; we began to live out the picture of ourselves we had created in our minds.

In time, we became what we most believed about ourselves. And in so doing, we created that wall of failure and self-doubt that for most of us will stand invisibly but powerfully between us and our unlimited future for as long as our old programming remains in force. Unless the programming we received is erased or replaced with different programming, it will stay with us permanently and affect and direct everything we do for the rest of our lives.

Fortunately, that doesn't have to be the case.

WHAT COULD YOUR FUTURE HOLD?

Because of important breakthroughs in the field of neuroscience, we are no longer at the mercy of our old programs and old conditioning that were never true about us in the first place. We can begin to truly live up to the unlimited potential each of us was born with, because we now understand how to rewire the brain, by taking control of the day-to-day, verbal programming process.

Think for a moment what you might do differently tomorrow if you were someone else—someone whose programming was different from yours. Or what might you do differently if you had been brought up with a completely different, more positive set of attitudes and beliefs and feelings from those that you may have now—attitudes and beliefs and feelings that, in every case, would assure you of having an abundance of self-belief, enthusiasm, and achievement?

If you had just the right kind of successful new mental programs, would you be doing the same thing for a living that you are doing now? Would you be doing your job in exactly the same way? What about your personal life? Would you change anything, improve anything? Would you have reached any more goals than you have reached? Would you have more money in the bank or any more financial security than you have now? What about your day-to-day life—would it be less frustrating and more rewarding? And, with different preparation or conditioning, what could your future hold? Would it be the same as your future holds for you today, or would it be better?

What if each and every day, from the time you were a small child, you had been given an extra helping of self-confidence, double the amount of determination, and twice the amount of belief in the outcome? Can you imagine what tasks you might accomplish more easily, what problems you would overcome, or what goals you could reach? After all, success, ultimately, is up to the individual. It isn't the pen—it's the writer; it isn't the road—it's the runner who counts.

Whatever age you are now, however many successes or failures you've had along the way, what if you could now change that old mental programming? What if you could physically rewire your brain? And what if you could do it in such a way that you could affect and improve your attitudes and your behavior quickly—not through years of difficult study or training, but easily and simply, anytime you chose to do so?

That is exactly what the brain will do.

We now know precisely how to change our old programming, and how to replace it with specific, word-for-word new programs. Those new programs, in time, lead to better brain wiring, which in turn leads to happier and more successful lives for all of us.

Our new understanding of the brain's neuroplasticity—its ability to rewire itself throughout our entire lifetime—is the understanding that can now help us make a vital change in the programming we accept from others, and what we say when we talk to ourselves. And when you decide to apply that new understanding to your everyday life in a simple, dedicated way, the unfilled promise at the end of your success journey can, at last, be realized.

CHAPTER THREE

Creating Positive Change That Lasts

Here is a short summary of the rules of success that have been given to us over the years. Each of these ideas is designed to help you create positive changes in your life. We've learned that if you want to be successful, you should:

- Believe In Yourself
- Keep Your Priorities Straight
- Take Responsibility For Yourself
- Create Your Own Future
- Meditate Daily
- Practice Mindfulness
- Focus On What You Want
- Attract What You Desire
- Learn To Visualize The Outcome Of Your Goals
- Never Let Anyone Control Your Destiny For You
- Be Creative
- Think Big
- Control Stress
- Be Aggressive And Assertive
- Think Positively
- Chart Your Own Course

- Set Specific Goals And Review Them Often
- Spend Some Time Each Day Improving Your Mind
- Review Your Results And Readjust As Necessary
- Be Tolerant
- Do Everything With Love
- Don't Hate
- Have Courage
- Recognize That Most Of What We Believe About Life Is An Illusion
- Be Honest
- Work Hard
- Believe Money Is Good And It Will Come To You
- Have Faith
- If You Agree To Do It, Enjoy It
- Be Strong
- Show Affection
- Manage Your Time
- Dress Right
- Learn To Sell Yourself
- Take Time Off
- Believe In A "Higher Self"
- Eat Right
- Live Prudently
- Seek The Aid Of Others Who Are In Sympathy With Your Goals
- Give Assistance To Others
- Keep Motivated
- Be Optimistic
- Trust Others And Be Worthy Of Trust
- Recognize That Success Is More Than Money
- Be Kind
- See The "Big Picture"

- Take Care Of The Details
- Get Organized
- Don't Procrastinate
- Stay In Control
- Keep Fit
- See Problems As "Opportunities"
- Learn Everything You Can About Your Job
- Don't Be Afraid Of Success
- Be Generous To Others
- Believe In God
- Reach A Little Higher Than You Thought You Could
- Set Your Sights
- Take Action
- Never Give Up

This list of self-improvement teachings suggests that we've been given most of the keys to success. If you follow those rules, you should create positive change, and by doing that, become successful.

Our new understanding of the brain's neuroplasticity, however, tells us that in order for these rules to work—or for the changes to become *permanent* changes—there are three essential ingredients that will ensure that the ideas will become a permanent part of you.

1. The first ingredient is: In order to work, and keep working, *the new idea (or message) has to become physically wired into your brain.* Unless the new messages or directions are actually wired into your brain's neural networks, even the best of the ideas will work only temporarily.
2. The second ingredient for creating lasting, positive mental changes is: *Understanding how your brain gets wired, and the*

role you play in the wiring process. An understanding of how your brain gets programmed puts you in direct control of the process of creating the change and making it last.

3. The third ingredient for creating positive personal change—which always begins with *mental* change—is: *A new, word-for-word set of directions, new programming to both your conscious and subconscious minds.* That means a specific "programming vocabulary" that is worded in a specific way, that anyone can use at any time, to replace the old negative programming with positive, productive new directions.

The only solution that includes all three of the essential ingredients that create lasting change in the brain is "self-talk."

Think for a moment of some of the things you would like to accomplish or achieve in your life—or even smaller things you would like to change about your life right now. Your objective could be to earn more income, have a better family life, improve your skills, do better in school, do better at work—anything at all.

Whatever means you choose to make the change, unless you first begin to change your old programming, the years of conditioning that keep you doing it the *old* way, the likely outcome is that what you want to accomplish will not work—or will not last.

When you use any of the personal growth ideas and concepts that are available to you, the practice of self-talk—the practice of consciously and actively rewiring your brain with a more successful, new picture of yourself—is the ingredient that programs your brain and changes your future. But bear in mind that as you do this, it is essential to program in the *right* new self-talk.

Whatever you put into your mind, in *one way or another,* is what you will get back out, in *one way or another.*

CHAPTER FOUR

New Discoveries

Neuroscientists have learned that much of what we had suspected about the human brain is true: The brain operates very much like a personal computer. It's not that simple, of course. For one thing, the brain is still many times more powerful, in some respects, than the most powerful computers we have yet created. Even though the adult human brain weighs only about sixteen hundred grams, about three pounds, and looks more like a lump of gray cauliflower than a desktop computer, the brain functions in some important ways much like the man-made computers that are patterned after it.

In nontechnical language, a typical computer has a few basic parts: a screen, a keyboard or touch screen, and a programming and storage device. Each of us has similar parts. In us, the computer's display screen is comparable to our appearance and our actions—what we "display" to the world around us. Our keyboard or input device is our five senses. Anything we hear, see, taste, touch, or smell—and anything we say to ourselves—is input to our brains through our five senses. A computer uses a device to record and store information. In our brains, the storage device is our subconscious mind. Messages we receive repeatedly are recorded and wired into our subconscious minds.

If you understand computers, my simplified explanation will be obvious and easy to understand. But an in-depth knowledge of computers isn't important; what matters most is knowing that whatever is programmed into your own personal "mental" computer is *permanently* programmed. That is, whatever programming you have received up to now is just as important and just as permanent as any program that has been typed into the most powerful man-made computers.

THE CONTROL CENTER

To help simplify the complex process of how and why the programming of the human brain affects us as much as it does, let's take a quick, imaginary look into the brain's central control room. That is the part of the brain where commands are received and where all the orders are handed out—the part of the brain that makes us feel good, work hard, and get things done. Or, when not so well directed, it makes us slow down, fear the outcome, and stop dead-still in our tracks.

Imagine standing in the control center of the brain, in front of a wall that is completely covered with literally tens of thousands of light switches, much like the light switches in our homes.

One section of switches controls our moods. Another section governs our health. Another group of switches controls our emotions, another our planning functions, another our hopes and dreams. Another section is responsible for how we act, how we move, sit, stand, walk, look, speak, react, and respond. Everything about us—our memory, our judgment, our attitude, our fears, our creativity, logic, and spirit—is controlled by the switches in our mental control room.

When any command is transmitted to the control room, the proper directions are sent to the appropriate panels of switches. Within a fraction of a second, some of those switches are turned off or turned on.

Within the brain itself, a network of tens of billions of neurons, and electrochemical switches called neurotransmitters, telegraph messages to every part of the brain, selecting just the right section of switches, which in turn switches parts of us "on" and parts of us "off."

The brain's infinitesimally small chemical receiving centers respond to almost imperceptible electrochemical signals that deliver nearly unmeasurable—but highly potent—chemical substances to our brain, our central nervous system, and to our bodies—which in turn control or affect everything we do.

It is the brain's responsibility to take care of us. It does so by constantly monitoring our needs and directing the various parts of our systems to take the necessary action. The brain automatically responds to every one of our unconscious electrical/chemical mental and physical commands—those that are principally concerned with keeping us alive.

THE BIOCHEMICAL ELECTRICAL IMPULSES CALLED "THOUGHTS"

It was in comparing the human brain to a computer that we were led to the first truly new breakthrough in our understanding of human behavior in many years. This breakthrough came when we discovered the direct link between our own thoughts and the physical wiring of neural pathways and networks in our brains.

We learned that the human brain responds strongest to a

special kind of command—key electrical impulses that also turn the switches in the brain on or off. Those electrical impulses, the special mental commands that direct us, control us, and wire neural networks into our brains, are called "thoughts."

Every thought we think, every conscious or unconscious thought we say to ourselves, is translated into electrical impulses in the brain, which in turn direct the control centers in our brains to electrically and chemically affect and control every motion, every feeling, every action we take, every moment of every day.

Whatever "thoughts" you programmed into your brain, or have allowed others to program into you, are affecting, directing, or controlling everything about you.

From the day we were born, we have received a staggering amount of programming, millions of messages in our lifetime. Some of the programming is obvious, but much of it we are never even aware of receiving.

The obvious programs are those comments, questions, and statements that are made to us directly. When we're young, we are told by our parents, and other adults, what we can and cannot do. We are told what we are good at and what we are not. We are told how we look. We are told what to expect, what to believe in, how to act, and what to do or not to do.

Because, starting out as children, completely dependent on others, it is important to our survival to listen and to believe what others say, and we learn to accept what others tell us. In time, with repetition, it is wired in—and we learn to believe it.

CHAPTER FIVE

We Learn to Believe

What adults tell us and what we learn to perceive about ourselves as children has an incredibly important effect on us. It informs what we believe about most of what is going on around us, and almost everything that we come to believe about ourselves.

I still remember the time when, as a middle-school student, I wanted more than anything I could think of to play a musical instrument and be a member of the school band. Along with ten or twelve other students from my class, I decided to try out for the band. After being handed a completely alien musical instrument and trying to get it to make music in front of the band instructor, my teacher, and the other students, I was dismissed.

I knew that I had not done well. But it was an hour later, after the last student of the day had performed, that I overheard the band director telling my teacher that not only could I not play in the band, but I also had no musical ability and would never be able to play an instrument. What incredible programming for a twelve-year-old boy who had his heart set on learning how to play!

It worked. I had heard from someone else that I had no musical ability, and I believed it. I accepted *as fact* that I had no musical talent, and that I never would. It wasn't until years later that I finally got up enough courage to rent a piano, learn some notes, and play it secretly when no one was around to remind me that I could not play. I never did develop the skill I wanted. But I learned, after some twenty frustrating years, that our school band director was wrong. And I had believed him.

Here is an opposite example. Michael, who at the age of six often visited the elderly gentleman next door for afternoon chats, was safely out of sight but within hearing distance at the top of the stairs one evening, ready for bed, when the neighbor stopped by. Little Michael overheard the old man tell his mother that Michael was very creative, and he knew that Mike would grow up to do things that were creative.

Decades later, Mike Vance would become dean of Disney University. Later, through his personal consulting and his work with major corporations and organizations throughout the world, he went on to become one of the premier creativity trainers in the United States. Little Michael, by accident, overheard one small "program" about himself. And Michael believed it.

Unfortunately, little of our own programming has done as much on our behalf. Can you imagine the number of times some child has heard the innocent but thoughtless words, "You'll never amount to much," or was told "that sport," "that career," "that mate," or "that dream" was not *right* for him or her? Just imagine what our eager and open young minds perceived and believed.

UNCONSCIOUS CONDITIONING FROM OTHERS

Some of our programming is obvious. But most of it is not; most of it has been much more subtle. Every day we receive an endless stream of commands, directives, controls, inducements, and expectations from others. Everything around us nudges, demands, or persuades. Even as adults, we are met with a torrent of influences; we are not even aware of most of them. We are ships with countless captains, all seeking to direct us on their own courses, for their own purposes, not even knowing they are leading our ships astray.

As long as you and I allow others to program us in a way that fits *their* choosing, we are, without a doubt, out of control, captive to the whims of some unknown destiny, not quite recognizing that what hangs in the balance is the fulfillment of our own futures.

Why do so many therapists take their patients back to a time in their childhood when the problem was first created? Because that is where the beliefs began. That is where the fear, the trauma, or the self-identity first began to take hold. Out of those early years, each of us formed a composite picture of ourselves. It made little difference whether the pictures of ourselves that we created were true or not. Our experiences, our acceptance of what we heard from others and what we told ourselves, became the foundation for the mental programming that directs us today.

Of course, not all of our past programming has been the wrong kind. Some of it has been good. Most of us have experienced the love and caring of others. And most of us have been touched from time to time with visions of positive self-belief. Many of us have had parents who countered their misgivings with encouragement. We have had coaches, teachers, and friends who saw the best in us. As we grew, all of us, from time to time, have had our successes.

But, at our best, we have been living with only a part of our life's programs working *for* us. Imagine what you could do if you could override the programs in your subconscious mind, those that still work against you, and replace them with a refreshing *new* set of programs of absolute belief, an almost unconscious, automatic new set of programs that would go to work for you—replacing the barriers with a refreshing new look at the life you have in front of you.

Think what you could do, beginning tomorrow, if the shackles of bad habits, old conditioning, and self-doubt were suddenly gone.

I once asked a woman who had lost 120 pounds what she felt like after succeeding in her goal to lose the weight. Her answer was, "I feel like I've lost a hundred and twenty pounds!" I understood her joy. Sometime, when you are at a health spa or gym, go over to the weight-lifting section and try to pick up 120 pounds.

And the mental weight we so often carry with us is far heavier to bear. Imagine losing, even for one day, all of the extra weight of self-doubt and disbelief we carry with us. Think how fast you could run.

Because of our brain's neuroplasticity, freedom of mind is possible, and not beyond the reach of any of us. Not only can you achieve that freedom for yourself, but we are about to see that there are a few practical steps you can take to make the freedom of a self-directed mind a permanent part of every day of your life.

You already have all of the necessary equipment. You were born with everything you need to live your life in a most exceptional and worthwhile way. It makes no difference what you have thought or what you have done in the past. From this day on, you can, if you choose, change a little to gain a lot.

YOUR PERSONAL ONBOARD COMPUTER

Earlier, we discussed how much of the programming each of us received was the wrong kind; that as much as 77 percent or more of everything that is recorded and stored in our subconscious minds is counterproductive and works against us—in short, that for the most part, we are wired *not* to succeed.

Let's say that I called you this evening and told you that I had just chartered an airplane to fly to Europe, and I was inviting you and your family or friends to join me. We are all going to go to Europe for a fabulous two-week vacation (all expenses paid, of course).

But now, let's say that just as we are boarding the plane, we overhear the first officer talking to the captain. We hear him tell the captain that the airplane's onboard computer—the computer that flies the plane—is *programmed wrong*. It has been programmed so that 77 percent of the directions that will control the plane are the wrong directions.

If you knew that the airplane's onboard computer was programmed wrong, what would you do next? You would get *off* the plane! You certainly wouldn't want to be on an airplane with bad computer programs. You would know that the plane would have to do one of two things: It would either land in the wrong place (not a happy thought while flying over the Atlantic), or it would *crash*.

And that is exactly the kind of programs most of us have. No wonder things don't work. No wonder we dream, hope, try, struggle, get by, fall short of the mark, or fail. No wonder we would like to get more out of life, solve some problems, or reach some goals—but can't seem to be able to. We've got a *bad* set of programs. *We have been trying to achieve our goals with our own onboard computer preprogrammed to hold us back—or fly us in the wrong direction.*

Do you want to live with *any* bad programs, much less the high percentage it is estimated most people carry around with them? Do you want to go through the rest of your life literally at the mercy of programs you don't want? You don't have to.

You can override almost any conditioning you have ever received, in any part of your life. It makes absolutely no difference who, where, what, why, or how you have been in the past. It makes no difference what you believed about yourself or what others may have believed about you. It makes no difference what circumstances life may have tossed in your lap. You can put yourself in control. Now it's your turn.

You can reprogram. You can rewire your life. You can erase the old negative, counterproductive, work-against-you programming and replace it with a healthy, new, positive, *productive* kind of programming.

We've now learned how to do that: *Rewire. Erase and replace.* And it all starts with learning how to talk to yourself.

A NEW SET OF DIRECTIONS

If we can change our attitudes and our behavior just by changing our programming, then none of us has to continue struggling through life with our old, negative programming dragging us down or holding us back. If we can just learn to give specific, productive new programming messages to our brains, then we have a chance to make things work—and keep working.

When you recognize that we can make a change in our lives by making a change in our programming, you see, for the first time, a crack in the wall of the 148,000 negatives, doubts, and destructive beliefs that each of us has built up in front of us. It becomes clear that what was holding us back, defeating us, can itself be defeated, and you realize that an exciting new future is about to become available to anyone who was standing behind the wall, waiting to get through.

What an exciting decision it is to break through that wall! Any of us can do it. Once we recognize what the real wall is, we can get past it.

CHAPTER SIX

The Wall

All of us talk to ourselves all of the time. Our self-talk may be in spoken words or unspoken thoughts. It can take the form of feelings, impressions, or even wordless physical responses, like the clutch in the stomach that comes when we are surprised or afraid, or the rush that comes with excitement or joy. We are thinking machines that never shut down. From childhood, we have been watching, listening to, sifting, sorting, analyzing, judging, cataloging, and storing everything that goes on about us.

Most of our self-talk is unconscious; we are not even aware of it. At times, our self-talk comes in feelings that can't quite be put into words. At other times, it comes in little flashes, flickers of thoughts that never quite catch fire or glow bright enough or last long enough to become ideas, clearly thought out and understood.

All of our thoughts, all of the pictures in our minds, are always tied to something else that we already know about. If you are given a new thought or a new picture, one you have never thought about or imagined before, your brain will immediately find something else in your mind to tie the new information to, to give it sense, to help you understand.

Every new thought you think has to have some old thoughts to stick to, a proper place to fit. When you are told something new, your brain will, in a fraction of a second, scan through literally millions of mental filing cabinets, filled with every idea or thought or impression you have ever stored. In that same fraction of a second, based on the information already stored in your mental files, your brain will send you an instant message, telling you how to feel about this new thought, where it should get filed, and whether you should accept and believe it, keep it and use it, or disapprove it, disbelieve it, and throw it out.

The more we believe about something, the more we will accept other ideas that are similar. The more files we have in our mental filing cabinets that tell us something about ourselves, the more we will attract and accept other thoughts and ideas that support and prove what is already stored in our files. The more you think about yourself in a certain way, the more you will think about yourself *in that same certain way.* The more you think about *anything* in a certain way, the more you will believe that *that* is how it really is. The mind works that way because the brain always tries to tie any *new* thing you think to something you already believe.

Understanding that makes it easy to see why it is hard to teach old dogs new tricks, change our minds, or unstick ourselves from the ideas we are solidly stuck in. It also tells us why the longer you believe something, the harder it is to change that belief. *The longer you have bought the thought, the "truer" it is.*

In our mental control centers, we fill to overflowing the files that support what we have told ourselves most, and we throw out anything that disagrees. And meanwhile, we keep ourselves busily, blissfully ignorant of something about us that could have made a difference in our lives—something about ourselves called "the truth."

A SELF-MADE WALL OF *NEGATIVE* SELF-TALK

While most self-talk is either unconscious or goes unnoticed, some self-talk is glaringly obvious and, not surprisingly, clearly self-defeating. Although some of the self-talk people use is constructive and beneficial, most of it is the opposite—the kind of self-talk that is counterproductive and self-defeating.

For a period of time during my quest for a more practical path to lasting self-improvement, to see just how pervasive negative self-talk might be, each time I heard an example of this kind of self-talk, I wrote it down. In time, my list included hundreds of self-talk statements that are made by people—every day. Most of the people who use negative self-talk are not aware of what they are saying. And few, if any, of them are aware of the power of the programming—the *negative* programming—they are giving themselves.

If everything you tell yourself *about yourself* becomes a directive to your subconscious mind, then anytime you make a statement about yourself that is negative, you are directing your subconscious mind to make you become the person you just described—negatively.

Here are just a few examples of frequently used *negative* self-talk. As you read them, see if you know someone who says something similar, or if you have said something like any of these yourself.

- I can't remember names.
- It's going to be another one of those days.
- It's just no use.
- I just know it won't work.
- Nothing ever goes right for me.

- That's just my luck.
- I'm so clumsy.
- I don't have the talent.
- I'm just not creative.
- Everything I eat goes right to my waist.
- I can't seem to get organized.
- Today just isn't my day.
- I can never afford the things I want.
- I already know I won't like it.
- No matter what I do I can't seem to lose weight.
- I never have enough time.
- I just don't have the patience for that.
- That really makes me mad.
- Another blue Monday.
- When will I ever learn.
- I get sick just thinking about it.
- Sometimes I just hate myself.
- I'm just no good.
- I'm too shy.
- I never know what to say.
- With my luck I don't have a chance.
- Things just aren't working out right for me.
- I don't have the energy I used to.
- I'm really out of shape.
- I never have any money left over at the end of the month.
- Why should I try, it's not going to work anyway.
- I've never been any good at that.
- My desk is always a mess.
- The only kind of luck I have is bad luck.
- I never win anything.
- I feel like I'm over the hill.

- Someone always beats me to it.
- Nobody likes me.
- I never get a break.
- It seems like I'm always broke.
- Everything I touch turns to *bleep*.
- Nobody wants to pay me what I'm worth.
- Sometimes I wish I'd never been born.
- I'm just no good at math.
- I lose weight but then I gain it right back again.
- I get so depressed.
- I just can't seem to get anything done.
- Nothing seems to go right for me.
- I'm just not a salesperson.
- That's impossible.
- There's just no way.
- I always freeze up in front of a group.
- I'm nothing without my first cup of coffee in the morning.
- I just can't get with it today.
- I'll never get it right.
- I just can't take it anymore.
- I hate my job.
- I get a cold this time every year.
- I'm just not cut out for that.
- I'm really at the end of my rope.
- You can't trust anyone anymore.
- I just can't handle this.
- I never seem to get anyplace on time.
- I've always been bad with words.
- If only I were smarter.
- If only I were taller.
- If only I had more time.

- If only I had more money.
- . . . and on, and on, and on.

Imagine sitting down at your personal computer keyboard and typing any one of those directions into the computer's permanent memory storage. And imagine that your computer will do whatever you program it to do.

That's exactly what we do to our brains. No wonder things go wrong. No wonder things don't work out right! If your mental computer—the one that flies your plane—is programmed with the wrong directions, *you cannot possibly be as successful as you would like to be;* you cannot get where you want to go.

LIVING WITH THE RESULTS

One day I was having lunch with a friend in a coffee shop located in a large convention hotel. While we were waiting for our lunch, we were discussing negative self-talk and commenting on how we end up becoming the result of what we say to ourselves. During our discussion, a perfect example of that very thing happened.

As our waitress approached our table with both arms filled with plates of food, she stumbled and dropped an armload of hot food on the table and floor in front of us, and exclaimed loudly, "Oh, I'm *so clumsy*!"

My friend and I had just witnessed a firsthand example of the result of the simplest kind of negative self-talk. I don't know how many times before that waitress had told herself she was clumsy. But she had undoubtedly said it to herself often enough to believe that it was true, and to make it happen.

As another example, let's take something as common as the

problem of not being able to remember names. For twenty-five years you may have said to yourself, "I can never remember names." Then one evening you go to a party. You are introduced to someone whose name you want to remember and you say to yourself, "I'm going to remember this person's name." What happens ten seconds later? You forget the name. Why? Because for the past twenty-five years you have been telling yourself that's what you'll do. You have been *programming* yourself to forget.

Minutes later, at the party, you find yourself standing there, a little embarrassed, mentally going through the alphabet, trying to remember the person's name. And meanwhile, as you're feeling forgetful and foolish, your subconscious, feeling very proud, is saying, *"See, I did what you told me to. I made you forget the name."*

If your self-talk, the directions you wire into your subconscious mind, will do that, don't you suppose it will do whatever else you tell it to do? If you were to reprogram someone strongly enough for them to believe that it was safe to drive up to an intersection and turn the wrong way into oncoming traffic, they would do it. *The human brain will do anything possible you tell it to do if you tell it often enough and strongly enough.* If you tell it the wrong thing about yourself, that is what it will accept—and act upon.

The subconscious mind does not see the difference between the statement that we are clumsy and the statement that we are graceful, well coordinated, and in control. It does not know the difference between being told that we are poor, and the statement that we are wealthy. It accepts our programming just as we give it.

Our internal programming mechanism treats anything we tell it with equal indifference. As a result, when we casually state,

"No matter what I do, I just can't seem to make enough money to make ends meet," our subconscious mind says, *"Okay, I'll do what you're telling me to do. I'll make sure you can't make ends meet."* In turn, it will unleash its powerful control over our mental and physical self to achieve the result it was told to accomplish.

I met one gentleman whom I would consider to be a fine man, but unfortunate. After twenty years of marriage, raising several children into their teens, and building a profitable business, he lost his wife to divorce, his children to the wife, and his business to his partners. What intrigued me about this man's story was that he talked only of his failures, his defeats, his downfall, and the problems he anticipated for his future. It was sad to see someone with his depth, his warmth, and his capabilities completely subjected to the failures he had long ago created for himself in his own mind.

As was the case with that individual, our brains will affect and influence what we do in every area of our lives, through that complex process of electrochemical physiological controls I described earlier. It will directly affect everything about us, from how we get along with someone at home to the amount of money we earn.

A typical example of this is our own self-accepted beliefs about our personal financial capabilities—or limitations. Unless we change the programs we gave to ourselves, the ones that told us we can't seem to earn enough money, our subconscious will successfully accomplish its programmed task of keeping us earning less than we would like. Had we given it the right programming, that same subconscious mind, instead of keeping us poor or of average means, would just as gladly have made us rich in every way.

CHAPTER SEVEN

Passing It On

Because we learned our programs from people around us, it is natural that we also pass the same kind of programming on to others. Unless we learn differently, we end up giving the same programming to our own children. I have collected dozens of examples of statements and comments that loving parents have told their children without once realizing that they were creating a self-belief in that child that would wire the children for *failure* instead of the happiness and success the parents were trying to bestow.

You may recognize some of these examples. Sincere, loving, caring parents, teachers, and friends have told children: *"You're just no good at that," "Your room is always a mess," "Can't you do anything right?" "You're just like your father," (which always seems to be said when the child has done something wrong), "Why can't you be more like your sister (or brother)?" "You'll never be an artist (or athlete, etc.)," "You just don't try," "You never listen to me," "I tell you to do something and you do just the opposite," "You never study," "Your grades are atrocious," "You talk too much," "You always hang around with the wrong kind of friends," "You don't even know where home is anymore," "You're lazy," "You don't care about anyone but yourself," "You're determined to cause problems,"*

"You just don't think," and so on. And some children, even while you are reading this, are being told the most assuredly destructive words, *"You'll never amount to anything."*

I suspect that some of what is said to children and teenagers behind closed doors may be even stronger than the few examples I have just given. But with that kind of programming, even in its most innocent and casual form, can you imagine how many times young, impressionable, unknowing children are told things that end up working against them—how many times we type a *bad* program into their personal computers?

Of course, much of what we say is said for the purpose of giving a child proper training, a proper "upbringing." But in so doing, by using words that program the child in the wrong way, we unwittingly help the child create a self-identity that believes that the negative things we are saying is "the truth"—we create a less than healthy portrait of how the child sees himself or herself inside, and eventually will become.

Think for a moment of the dreams you *know* you could have accomplished in your own life; think of the talents and skills already within you that could have been developed into lasting achievements, if you'd just had the right amount of self-belief—the belief that you *could* instead of the belief that you could *not.* Most of us, if given a magic wand that when waved could fulfill any of our dreams, would most certainly make some changes in our lives.

All of us have had the dreams. All of us deserve to see our dreams come true. Were it not for the brick wall of bad programming that stands in our way, each of us, each day, would be living out more of those dreams, reaching heights of attainment we seldom even dream of.

We are fortunate to be living at a time when we are beginning to understand what goes on inside that incredible mechanism we call a brain. By unlocking more and more of its secrets, we have learned that we have a *personal* vote in the outcome of our own destiny.

We have learned that what we put into our brains is what we will get back out. We also have learned that the subconscious mind is a sponge; it will believe anything you tell it—it will even believe a lie—if you tell it often enough and strongly enough. That part of the brain makes no moral judgments; it simply accepts what you tell it.

Your tablet or your desktop computer doesn't care what is typed into it. It never questions whether you are telling it the truth or not. It just accepts and acts upon whatever you program into it. And as with that computer, it makes no difference whether the things you have told yourself or believed about yourself in the past were true or not. *The brain doesn't care.*

THE MACHINE THAT NEVER SLEEPS

Your subconscious mind is working right now. It is working day and night, to make sure that you become precisely the person you have *unconsciously* described yourself to be. If your programs picture you as having trouble earning enough income, your subconscious mind is doing everything it can, right now, to make sure that you have trouble earning more money. If you have conditioned yourself to believe that you can't stick to a diet, you can be sure that your subconscious mind will make *sure* that no diet will work for you—at least not for long. Your subconscious can only do for you what you (and others) tell it to do.

In a previous chapter, I pointed out that during the formative years of our lives, each of us is told "No," or what we *cannot* do, many thousands of times. Each of those "cannots" was a directive to our subconscious minds.

And as we, because of our conditioning, began to follow suit and say similar "cannots" to ourselves, we fell into the unconscious habit of programming ourselves in the same wrong way as did our parents, friends, and others around us. And right now, at this moment, each of our subconscious minds is working to make sure we become just as those tens of thousands of negative directives programmed us to be.

Since that time, of course, we have continued to give ourselves new programs. The examples of negative statements I gave you earlier are only a few leaves in a forest of negative self-talk. In fact, most of our average, habit-formed, everyday self-talk is the kind that we don't even notice. It is the kind that we say to ourselves silently, often without words. Much of our self-talk is made up of the quiet nudges of self-doubt, the unspoken fears of little (or grand) failures, and the nagging discomfort of knowing that things aren't right.

When we talk to our friends, it sometimes seems easier to talk about problems than about exciting potential. Our daily conversation scripts often sound like they were written by the same editors who write the headlines for the latest viral bad news story. We live, in our poorly programmed unconscious minds, in the disquieting shadow-world of uncertainty—believing that we should be achieving, but not knowing why, after so much frustration and trying, we are not.

By the time most of us reach adulthood, we are so conditioned to think in a certain way that our pattern of self-talk becomes habit that is physically wired into our brains. It is fixed. And for most, it remains that way. How we look at life, what we believe about ourselves, how we view *anything,* and what we do about it, gets filtered through our preconceptions.

We have told ourselves over and over, consciously and unconsciously, what does not work. In the past, too often we learned to automatically believe *the worst first, and the best last.* But now we have learned that it does not have to be that way. There is something, starting right now, that you can do about it. It is the key to how you manage yourself, and how you live and manage the rest of your life.

CHAPTER EIGHT

The Self-Management Sequence

There is a natural process by which success or failure in managing or controlling our lives takes place. The process consists of a sequence of steps. If we are aware of what the steps are, we can improve our chances, and accelerate our advances. If we are not aware of what is causing our success, or foiling it, we end up at the mercy of chance. Life is not a matter of luck or fortune. We are not playing our lives out at a gaming table. If we leave our lives up to chance, chances are, we'll fail.

That is because success is always the *result* of something else, something that leads up to it. Now, we know that there are times when it looks like something good that happens is just an "accident." But there are those who would argue that *nothing* ever happens by accident—that everything that occurs in our lives does so because of what we mentally "create" to happen. Most of what seems to happen *to* you, happens *because of* you—something you created, directed, influenced, or allowed to happen.

Let's take your personal successes or failures on an average. Whether you are examining your smaller, everyday achievements, or the bigger monthly or yearly successes, by and large, on the average, those achievements and successes were not accidental. They were the result of something else.

The same is true of those things you did that didn't work out so well. On the average, the failures, too, were the results of something else—and that something else, in most cases, whether you succeeded or failed—was *you.* Something you did (or did not do) was the cause of that success or failure. Here's how it works.

THE SELF-MANAGEMENT SEQUENCE

The Five Steps That Control Our Success or Failure

1. BEHAVIOR

The step that most *directly* controls our success or failure is our behavior—what we do or do not do. Behavior means our *actions.* How we act, what we do, each moment of each day will determine whether or not we will be successful that moment or that day in anything that we do. The right series of the right actions will always end up making things work better than the wrong series of the wrong actions. In most cases, if you do the right thing, you're going to achieve the right results.

This step involves even the simplest level of behavior. As an example, if you like your job, do the right thing at the right time, and keep at it, there is a good chance that your job will do well for you. If, on the other hand, you do not like your work and do things that work against you on the job, it won't work as well for you.

Let's use another example. If a student in school refuses to study, never pays attention, and misses a lot of classes (all behavior), will the student do well in school? Probably not. If that student behaves in a way that says, "I don't like being where I am," his or her behavior will ultimately cause a problem. The good grades won't show up, and if something doesn't change, eventually neither will the student.

The same is true of your home life. If you don't like where you are in your home life, what will you do? If you are like most of us, in one way or another, your behavior, your actions will alert those around you that you are unhappy. The result will be an unhappy home life, or at a minimum you will have to live with disagreements, arguments, and unhappiness in one form or another.

On the other hand, if your actions are those that work *for* you instead of against you, the likelihood is that things around you will have a better chance of working for you instead of against you.

But it goes far beyond that. How you manage your "self," what you do, how you act each and every moment, every word you speak, motion you make, and action you take or do not take will determine how well anything in your life works for you. It does not take a wizard to tell us that when we do the *right* things, there is always a better chance that things will work better for us than when we do the *wrong* things.

But why do we do what we do? Why do we *not* do the things we know we should, and so often say and do things that we know we should *not*? What makes us do what we do? What makes us act the way we act, behave the way we behave? Why do we ever do *anything* that works against us instead of always doing exactly that which works *for* us? Is it because we don't know any better? No. We usually know what's right and what's wrong.

The reason we don't heed even our own advice is because of something else that affects, directs, influences, or controls all of our actions. That something that makes us do what we do is called our:

2. FEELINGS

Every action we take is first filtered through our feelings. How we *feel* about something will always determine or affect what we *do* and how well we do it.

If we feel good or positive about something, we will behave more positively about it. Our feelings will directly influence our actions. Have you ever watched children who were made to eat something they didn't like? How did they act? I've seen children who looked as though they were going to die right there on the spot. But set a favorite dessert in front of the same children and what will they do? They may look as though they're going to dive into it headfirst.

What is the difference between the one plate of food and the other? It's *not* that one type of food is better than the other. The difference is in how those children have come to *feel* about the food. The way the children felt determined what action they took. In *one* instance they fought it; in the other they relished it.

I have a friend whose worst fear is that of flying. Ordinarily, she is levelheaded and possesses an even disposition. But because of her fear of being in an airplane, she would rather drive a car from her home in the Midwest to visit her family on the East Coast, and lose two or three days getting there, than hop on a plane and be with her family in two or three short hours. When circumstances demand that she does fly, she loses her well-mannered, even temperament, her stress level triples, her anxieties take over, and she gets sick even before the flight begins.

Is it the flying? No. It is her *feelings* about flying that cause her to act the way she does. In this example, you'll notice that, once again, it made no difference if the individual's feelings were "rational"; her feelings nonetheless directly controlled, influenced, and severely affected the woman's actions.

Your feelings about anything you do will affect how you do it. It doesn't have to be feelings of like or dislike, joy or fear; *all* of your feelings affect your actions. How you feel about your job, your mate, your family, your money, your health, yourself, and your success will determine how you behave in each of these areas. If your feelings are positive and productive, your actions will follow.

But what causes you to *have* the feelings that are so much a part of you? Did you get them by accident? What creates the way you feel about anything? Chance? Never. Your feelings are created, controlled, determined, or influenced by your:

3. ATTITUDES

Your attitudes are the perspectives from which you view life. Some people seem to have a good attitude about most things. Some people seem to have a bad attitude about everything. But when you look closer, you will find that most of us have a combination of attitudes, some good, some not so good.

Whatever attitude we have about anything will affect how we feel about it, which in turn determines how we'll act about it, and that in turn determines whether or not we will do well. So our attitudes play a very important part in helping us become successful.

In fact, as we can see, a good attitude is *essential* to achievement of any kind. We so often hear of someone who is said to have a "bad attitude." The term is often applied to young people, especially to teenagers who frequently get into trouble, but we often hear it about adults, too. The implication is always that the individuals in question are not going to make it if they don't change their attitudes.

I would agree. Without a good attitude, a perspective that allows us to see the opportunities ahead and set our sights to reach them, we never will. But even more important is the fact that in order to possess the kinds of feelings that work *for* us, we've got to have the right attitudes to start with.

But where do we get our attitudes? Are we born with them? Or do they just appear out of nowhere?

Our attitudes are no accident. They don't just *happen*. Our attitudes are created, controlled, or influenced entirely by our:

4. BELIEFS

What we *believe* about anything will determine our attitudes about it, create our feelings, direct our actions, and in each instance, help us to do well or poorly, succeed or fail. The belief that we have about anything is so powerful that it can even make something appear to be something *different* than what it really is. "Belief" does not require that something actually be the way we see it to be. It only requires us to believe that that's the way it is.

Belief does not require something to be true. It only requires us to *believe that it's true*. That's powerful stuff! That means most of what reality is, to each of us, is based on what we have come to believe—whether it's true or not.

It is possible that tomorrow morning, in some classroom in a foreign nation, there will sit a little boy or girl who believes that *our* country is bad. It is also likely that tomorrow morning, in some classroom in our country, there will sit a young boy or girl who believes that the *other* nation is bad. It makes no difference whether it is true or not. It is what they believe. And what they believe will affect their attitudes, feelings, and actions. One day when they grow older, they could see each other as an enemy, and try to kill each other. To each of them it would be right. It would be what they believe.

When I was a child, sitting on a church bench, trying to understand what the man in the pulpit was talking about, I remember him telling us to "believe." I didn't know how to do that. I thought that some people were lucky and some were not. Some just naturally got to believe, and some didn't. I did not know yet where belief comes from, and I certainly didn't know the power that belief would have in my life and the power beliefs had held in the lives of every human being who had ever lived.

As an example of how important belief can be, imagine believing something about yourself, something that was working against you but that was not true.

Let's say you believed that you had trouble making friends easily, or being accepted easily and naturally by others. You believed you took a social backseat to people who seemed to be more popular. As a result, you found yourself standing back at social gatherings, self-conscious and unsure of what to say. At your work you often missed opportunities because you did not speak up—even when your idea was better than the idea that was accepted from someone else who did speak up. Let's say you knew that you wanted to be intelligent and witty and fun, but you believed that the *outside* you just didn't measure *up*.

Since whatever you believe about yourself will end up affecting what you do, you can be sure that if you believe that you are not as socially successful as you would like to be, your *belief* about yourself will turn out to be correct—whether it was true or not. Beyond tendencies toward assertiveness or shyness, et cetera, most social behaviors are conditioned to begin with—no one is born popular and socially adept. Every social grace, skill, and comfort level that we have, successful or unsuccessful, is based on what we learn to believe about ourselves. If you tell yourself that you *cannot,* what can the only outcome be?

We all have thousands of big and little beliefs about ourselves. Some of them probably are true. I suspect that most of them are not. But your mind will act as though they are true, if you believe them.

What makes us believe? Do our beliefs just one day spring out of nowhere? Were our beliefs handed to us on the day of our birth, like birthmarks of our heredity to be kept forever? Do we create them ourselves? Where do we get them? Our beliefs are not accidents of nature. Our beliefs are created and directed entirely by our:

5. PROGRAMMING

We believe what we are *programmed* to believe. Our conditioning, from the day we were born, has created, reinforced, and nearly permanently cemented most of what we believe about ourselves and what we believe about most of what goes on around us. Whether the programming was right or wrong, true or false, the result of it is what we believe.

It all starts with our programming. What we have accepted from the outside world, or fed to ourselves, has initiated a natural cause-and-effect chain reaction sequence that leads us either to successful self-management, or to the unsuccessful mismanagement of ourselves, our resources, and our future.

It is our programming that sets up our beliefs, and the chain reaction begins. In logical progression, what we believe determines our attitudes, affects our feelings, directs our behavior, and determines our success or failure.

1. *Programming creates beliefs.*
2. *Beliefs create attitudes.*

3. *Attitudes create feelings.*
4. *Feelings determine actions.*
5. *Actions create results.*

That's how the brain works. If you want to manage yourself in a better way, and change your results, you can do so at any time you choose. Start with the first step. Change your programming.

CHAPTER NINE

The Five Levels of Self-Talk

What is self-talk, and how does it work? The definition of self-talk, as we're using it throughout this book, can be simply stated: Self-talk is a way to override our past negative programming by erasing or replacing it with conscious, new positive directions. Self-talk is a practical way to live our lives by active intent rather than by passive acceptance.

With self-talk, we have a way to give new directions to our subconscious minds by talking to ourselves in a different way, consciously reprogramming our internal control centers with words and statements that are more effective, more helpful to every part of us that we would like to improve. The self-talk statements paint a new internal picture of ourselves as we would most like to be.

Self-talk gives each of us a way to change what we would like to change, even if we haven't been able to do so in the past. It offers us the chance to stop being the old self and start being a different, better self, a self that is no longer the product of conditioned response but governed instead by personal choice.

Actually, there are several kinds of self-talk. Each of us, each day, may use any of five different levels of self-talk. Each level is specific and distinct from the others. Some of the levels work for us, and some work against us. The more you know about each of them, the faster and more easily you will be able to master using the *right* kind of self-talk for yourself.

LEVEL 1 SELF-TALK

The Level of Negative Acceptance

("I can't . . .")

The five levels of self-talk start at the lowest, least beneficial level. At the bottom of the list—and the most harmful self-talk we can use—is Level 1, the level of Negative Acceptance. That is self-talk by which you say something bad or negative about yourself, and you accept it.

Earlier, we discussed several dozen commonly used self-talk statements and phrases. All of them were Level 1 self-talk. This level is easy to spot. It is almost always characterized by the words, "I can't . . ." or "If only I could . . ." or "I wish I could . . ." and so on. All Level 1 self-talk works against us. And unfortunately, it is the most frequently used self-talk of all.

"I just don't have the energy I used to," "I could never do that," "I just can't seem to lose weight," "Well, I just don't know," "Today's just not my day," and "I just can't" are typical of the kinds of doubts, fears, misgivings, and hesitations we program ourselves with when we say any Level 1 self-talk phrase to ourselves, out loud, silently, or to someone else. Remember, the subconscious mind is listening and waiting for our instructions, and it doesn't care what we tell it; it just does what we instruct it to do!

Level 1 self-talk represents everything from our simplest misgivings to the worst fears we have about ourselves. It is our way of telling ourselves to hesitate, question our capabilities, and accept less than we know we could have done, had we only given ourselves a chance. It is our way of timidly hiding in the shadows instead of boldly thriving in the sunshine.

There is no way to estimate the amount of havoc and misdirection that Level 1 self-talk wreaks in our lives. It clutters, blocks, and confuses. It turns self-assurance into self-doubt and chaos. It cripples our best intentions and seduces us into becoming satisfied with mediocrity. It is the heart of a "get by" attitude, its subtle whispers telling us to passively accept a fate far less great than we had once dreamed of attaining. It is the mythical siren that draws us onto the shore, dashing our hopes on reefs of despair and complacency.

Imagine going through your life using that kind of self-talk on yourself! When you think about it, why would anyone (once they know) want to use any self-talk that would program them to fail or do less than they could? Yet that is exactly what most of us have done.

It makes no difference how harmless the words seem at the time; they are the backbone of everything that works against us and stands in our way. Rid yourself of the negative "I can't" of Level 1 self-talk, and you will have rid yourself of your greatest foe.

LEVEL 2 SELF-TALK

The Level of Recognition—and Need to Change

("I need to . . ." "I should . . .")

This level is beguiling. On the surface, it looks as though it should work for us. But instead, it works against us. In this level of self-talk, we are stating to ourselves and to others our recognition of our need to change.

Level 2 self-talk is characterized by words such as "I need to . . ." or "I ought to . . ." or "I should . . ." Why does that work against us? Because it recognizes a problem, but creates no solution. When you say to yourself (or to someone else), "I really need to get more organized," what are you really saying? You are saying, "I really need to get more organized . . . but I'm not." When you complete the sentence, it is always, unconsciously, ended with an unspoken but still programmed Level 1 statement of negative self-talk.

"I really should try to get to work on time." "I've just got to lose some weight!" "I've got to do something about that." "I really ought to take more time with my kids." "I know I should study harder." Anytime you hear yourself telling yourself any Level 2 self-talk, stop for a moment and complete the sentence—finish, out loud, the program you are actually directing to your subconscious mind.

Your self-talk then becomes, "I'd really like to earn more income . . . but I'm *not*. I wish I could . . . but I *can't*. I know I need to take care of that . . . but I'm *not* taking care of it. I ought to call home more often . . . but I *don't*. I'd like things to work out better . . . but they *won't*."

Those are the directives we unwittingly give to ourselves. Those are the seemingly innocent but exceptionally effective programs we feed to the most powerful control center known to man. Instead of giving birth to dreams and accomplishments, Level 2 self-talk creates guilt, disappointment, and an acceptance of our own self-imagined inadequacies. Is that good programming? No, it isn't. Will it help you succeed? No, it will not.

LEVEL 3 SELF-TALK

The Level of Decision to Change

("I never . . ." "I no longer . . .")

Level 3 self-talk is the first level of self-talk that works *for* you instead of against you. In this level, you recognize the need to change, but you also make the decision to do something about it—and you state the decision in the present tense—as though the change has already taken place.

Level 3 is characterized by the words "I never," or "I no longer." In this level, you say, "I no longer have a problem dealing with people at work." "I never eat more than I should." "I never get upset in traffic." "I no longer put off doing anything I want to get done."

When you move to Level 3, you are automatically beginning to rephrase old negative "cannots," putting them behind you, and stating them in a new positive way that tells your subconscious mind to wake up, get moving, and make the change.

When you begin to practice the new self-talk for yourself, you will find that you will need to use Level 3 self-talk only on those occasions when you are working at effecting a specific change.

Let's use the example of someone who smokes, but who really wants to quit. If you have been a smoker and want to quit, you may want to try this yourself. Let's say that you smoke, but you finally decide that you want to stop smoking for good. So you begin by using Level 3 self-talk. You say to yourself, "I never smoke!" "I no longer enjoy smoking and I have quit." You use your new self-talk silently to yourself, but you also say it out loud, even when you are with other people. Until now, when you felt like lighting a cigarette, you would simply do so, think nothing about it, and say nothing about it.

But now, when you light a cigarette, you say out loud, "I never smoke." The first thing that will happen is that if you say those words in front of someone else, while you are lighting your cigarette, your friends are going to think you're a little strange! But you continue to say the words, both to yourself and out loud. And for a while, you continue to smoke, just as you have become conditioned to smoking, but you also continue to give yourself new self-talk at the same time: "I never smoke . . ." "I no longer smoke . . ." et cetera.

In not too long a time, what will happen? One day, you will be lighting a cigarette and saying, "I never smoke," and your subconscious mind is going to say, *"Then what are you doing with that little white thing in your hand? And one end of it is on fire!"*

You have been giving new programming to your subconscious, telling yourself that you no longer need to smoke. And your subconscious mind will automatically react by making sure that you no longer smoke. That's what you have started telling it to do.

There is, of course, more to self-talk than just a few simple words. Many habits have been years in the making and require a solid program of new self-talk to break them down and replace them. (How to do that is discussed in a later chapter.)

Whether the habit you are working to change is with your health, your relationships, your finances, or any other issue, it doesn't make any difference that you're still living out the results of the old, outdated habit when you start telling your subconscious that you choose to change.

Remember, the subconscious mind will believe anything you tell it if you tell it long enough and strongly enough. It will simply go to work to carry out its new directives. Your subconscious mind will receive the new direction, create a new, more successful picture of you in your control center, and, over time, will convince you to put the cigarette out, put down the fork instead of eating that extra dessert, or close your mouth before you shout those angry words at a coworker or loved one.

You no longer choose to maintain the habit that worked against your actions and your success. You choose to replace it with something better. That's exactly what you told your subconscious mind, so that's exactly what it will do. When the new programming takes over, it won't be the result of magic or luck. That's just the way the mind works. It works because you tell it what to do. Learn to tell it in the right way, and repeat it often enough, and the results will follow.

LEVEL 4 SELF-TALK

The Level of the Better You

("I am")

This is the most effective kind of self-talk we can ever use. In our self-talk vocabulary, Level 4 is the kind of self-talk that is needed most. It is at this level that you are painting a completed new picture of yourself, the way you really want to be, handing it to your subconscious, and saying, "This is the 'me' I want you to create. Forget all that bad programming I gave you in the past. This is your new program. Now let's get to work at it."

Level 4 self-talk is characterized by the words, "I am . . ."

"I am organized and in control of my life. I am a winner. I am healthy, energetic, enthusiastic, and I'm going for it. Nothing can stop me now. I like who I am. I am in tune, on top, and in touch, and going for it. I have determination, drive, and self-belief. I am living the life I choose, and I choose what's right."

You'll notice that, once again, this self-talk is stated in the present tense. Always keep in mind that by stating your self-talk in the present tense, you're not trying to kid yourself, or tell yourself something that isn't true. What you're actually doing is giving your brain a completed picture of the task. In essence you're saying, "This is how I choose to be. This is who I want you to help me become."

Instead of struggling with the past Level 1 self-talk, the Level 4 self-talker deals with problems and opportunities in a whole new, productive, self-activating way. The past procrastinator, who had been programmed to put things off, now says, "I do everything I need to do when I need to do it. I enjoy getting things done, and I enjoy doing things on time and in just the right way." The past problem is turned around to begin creating ongoing daily success.

Instead of saying, "I can never remember names," the Level 4 self-talker automatically says, "I have a great memory. People are important to me, and I am able to remember any name I choose to remember, anytime I want."

Level 4 self-talk is the positive self-talk that is the opposite of Level 1. It replaces helpless "cannots" with vibrant "Yes, I cans." Level 4 self-talk inspires, encourages, urges, and implores. It tugs at our hearts, touches our hopes, and paints in the pictures that color our dreams. It excites, demands, and pushes us forward. It strengthens the armor of our spirit and hardens the steel of our determination.

This is the self-talk that challenges us to do battle with our fears and end up the victor. It is the self-talk that stirs us to action, fills us up with self-belief, and plants our feet firmly on the solid bedrock of success.

Name the adversary, state the problem, and you can find the self-talk that created it. But for every word of negative self-talk that has ever been uttered, there is the right kind of self-talk to counter it, reprogram, fix the problem, and make it right.

Even reading the simplest examples of this special, powerful, reprogramming Level 4 self-talk makes you want to go for it: "I am a winner! I believe in myself. I respect myself and I like who I am. I have made the decision to win in my life, and that's what I'm doing!" Can you imagine going through the rest of your life with that kind of self-talk on your side? Think of the programming that kind of direction would create! It is yours for the taking. It is yours the moment you decide to choose a better way. You deserve the best out of life, and it's time to do something about it.

LEVEL 5 SELF-TALK

The Level of Universal Affirmation

("It is . . .")

There is another type of self-talk-like phrases called "Level 5 self-talk" that, while similar to the other levels of self-talk we're discussing, in practice is very different. This is the use of "affirmations."

Various forms of spiritually oriented affirmations have been practiced for many years. These affirmations are often similar to the mantras of the ancient religions that inspired them, and they usually affirm a oneness with spirit, or speak of a divine affinity of being that transcends our earthly life and gives greater meaning to our existence. This form of spiritual affirmation is characterized by the words, "It is . . ." such as, "I am one with the universe, and it is one with me. I am of it, within it, and exist as a shining spark of light in a firmament of divine goodness."

They are beautiful words, and they are meaningful. But lest I sound as though I am giving this level of self-talk less than its due, let me say only that those whose quest has placed them at this level already know. They don't need to read this book to learn that this type of self-talk-like wording, to them "affirmations," will serve as mantras to help them achieve their rather special goals.

It is still important, however, that we take care today of the things that are required today. And the everyday, practical kind of self-talk we're focusing on here is a different thing. As an example, affirmations are often associated with New Age thought; self-talk isn't. Affirmations typically have a metaphysical association; self-talk doesn't. Some authors, however, use the terms "self-talk" and "affirmations" interchangeably, and as a result, people are often confused by the terms.

To un-confuse the reader, here are my definitions:

Affirmation: A usually spiritually oriented phrase, often general in nature, that affirms an overriding consciousness of unity and well-being.

Self-Talk: Specific statements of self-direction designed to wire new neural pathways into the brain.

Affirmations can be wonderful, and anyone who chooses to use them should do so. But for our purposes, we will focus on the positive self-talk that will get you to work on time, help you get fit, help you earn more income, improve your attitude, strengthen your family ties, give yourself the self-image you deserve, and get the basic things in *this* life in order.

YOU CAN BEGIN RIGHT NOW

There are two levels of self-talk that you should learn first—and two others that you should unlearn fast. Starting right now, the moment you recognize why the self-talk you have used at Levels 1 and 2 hasn't worked, stop using it. There's no reason to use it any longer. Replace those two negative kinds of self-talk with the positive self-talk of Level 3 and Level 4.

If you'd like to start working at it right now, reread the section on Level 4. That's the self-talk that will get you going, change what you want to change, and get you headed on a journey that will take you toward the fulfillment of your dreams—and away from the frustrating roadblocks that have been standing in your way.

CHAPTER TEN

A New Look at Positive Thinking

At one time, after Norman Vincent Peale's best-selling book *The Power of Positive Thinking* first popularized the concept of positive thinking, many scientists and even some psychologists dismissed the idea, saying that positive thinking was no more than wishful thinking or self-delusion.

But later, because of scientific breakthroughs in brain scanning and imaging technology, when neuroscientists were finally able to study the neuron structure of specific areas of the brain, researchers discovered something that actually *proved* the efficacy of positive thinking—from a scientific point of view.

The researchers discovered that people who typically think positively *actually grow more neurons* in the left prefrontal cortex of their brain. That area of the brain is, in part, responsible for our ability to seek alternative solutions to problems, deal with challenges, and maintain an even balance. The research showed that the value of a "can do" spirit of positive thinking has, at its core, an important basis in the neuron structure of the brain itself.

Knowing that people who think more positively grow more neurons in their left prefrontal cortex tells us that instead of being wishful thinking, positive thinking actually increases neuron growth and activity in an area of the brain that is essential to having a healthy attitude, being open to possibilities, finding solutions, and creating successes.

Meanwhile, researchers found that people whose thinking is typically *negative* grow more neurons in the right prefrontal cortex of their brains. That's the part of the brain where pessimism, uncertainty, and negative moods live.

People who are "up" and positive spend more time in the *left* prefrontal cortex of their brains. People who are negative spend more time in the *right* prefrontal cortex of their brains. (One study showed that babies who cried when they were briefly separated from their mothers had a dominant right prefrontal cortex, while babies who stayed calm had a dominant left prefrontal cortex.)

The more time you spend in either the left or right prefrontal cortex of your brain—that is, the more time you spend being positive or negative—the more neurons you will grow in that area of the brain, and the more dominant that area will become. (This is why people who have the habit of being negative usually stay that way. They have grown more neurons in the "negative" part of their brain, so that part of their brain becomes dominant.)

THE CHALLENGES TO CHANGING

There are two challenges in changing from thinking negatively to thinking positively. The first challenge confronts those who believe that positive thinking, by itself, fixes everything. It doesn't. Just "believing" everything will work out, without creating an action plan to solve the problem, will only end in disappointment, and any notion of becoming a true positive thinker will soon fade away. (We even have a term for thinking that is *too* positive: Pollyanna thinking.) But the kind of positive thinking, and the positive self-talk we're talking about in this book, is also *responsible* thinking. It may be optimistic, but it is also practical and realistic. Thanks to the left prefrontal cortex, your brain looks for the best solution until it finds it.

The second challenge in changing from negative thinking to positive thinking is that just telling yourself you're going to be more positive in the future doesn't automatically rewire your brain to be that way. You can set a goal to be more optimistic, and to never be negative again, but that goal will only work if you take the time to rewire your brain with new positive programs. Here's how it works.

YOUR MENTAL APARTMENT

Imagine that you have a "mental apartment"—the place you live with your thoughts. That mental apartment is furnished with everything you think about yourself and the world around you; it is furnished with your thoughts.

Much of the mental furniture in this mental apartment is "hand-me-down" furniture. It is the old negative way of thinking that was handed down to us from our parents, our friends, our teachers, and everyone else who has been helping us program our subconscious minds: They gave us the furniture that we have kept and that we use in our mental apartment.

Imagine that most of that "furniture" (our negative thinking), because it was hand-me-down furniture, is weary with age. The old tattered sofa is sagging and worn. The chairs are broken and shaky, ready to fall apart if sat in too heavily. The pictures, hanging crookedly on the walls, are yellowed and faded.

The kitchen table leans at an angle, and the dishes are chipped and cracked; no cup has a handle because they have long since broken away. Coils of bedsprings show through, rusted and bent. The rug on the floor is more patches and holes than it is rug. In these furnishings, a strong new piece of furniture (some positive thought) would seem out of place, but though here and there there might be a sturdy piece of furniture or two, they are too overrun in the clutter to be noticed at all.

Now, let us say that I come over to your home, this mental apartment, and help you get rid of all the old furniture. I tell you that I am going to help you get rid of your old *negative* thinking once and for all. So, at four-thirty tomorrow afternoon I arrive, and we begin to carry all of your old hand-me-down furniture outside and we store it in the garage. We remove every piece, every dish, every rug, table, bed, sofa, and chair. We take out every old negative self-belief and store it away, safely out of sight.

By six o'clock that evening we have finished, and after I leave, you stand by yourself in the middle of your mental apartment. It is empty and spotless. There is not a negative thought, not a sofa, a picture, a book, or a chair in sight. You look around and think, *This is great. I've gotten rid of all of my old negative thinking. Now I can be a positive thinker.*

That's at six o'clock. You stand around, walk through your mental apartment, and then stand around some more. A little later that evening, after spending an hour or two with nothing but yourself and an empty apartment, what do you suppose you will do? You will go out into the garage, where the old furniture is stored, and get a chair. A little later, you will make another trip to the garage and bring in a table, and maybe a dish or two.

We are most comfortable with the thoughts we have lived with the most. It makes no difference if those thoughts aren't the best for us—it's what we know, it's what we are most secure in keeping at our side. By nine o'clock you may even have retrieved the trusty old TV. One by one, you will begin to *bring your old trusted and timeworn negative thoughts back into your mental apartment.* Why? Because when I helped you remove the old furniture, I didn't give you any *new* furniture to replace it with—I didn't give you any *positive* new thoughts to replace the negative old thoughts.

When you decide to stop thinking negatively, and do not have an immediate, new positive vocabulary to replace the old, you will always return to the comfortable old negative self-talk of the past. If you got rid of your old furniture and stored it in the garage, and you had no new furniture to replace it with, if I were to visit you again in three weeks, you would have all of your old furniture back in your apartment. You would probably have rearranged it to make it look fresh, but it would be the same old furniture, the same old programming you had in the first place.

REPLACE THE OLD WITH THE NEW

So instead, let us say that I knock on your door, and I ask you to come outside. There stands a shiny new delivery truck full of the most beautiful furniture you have ever imagined. For the next two or three hours I help you carry all of the beautiful new furniture, your new positive self-talk, into your mental apartment. And this time, we don't store the old negative furniture in the garage; we pile it up and set a match to it. We get rid of it. Don't give your old furniture to someone *else—don't pass along your negative self-talk to someone else. After all, that's how you got it in the first place.*

This time when I leave, you walk through your mental apartment and look around you. What an incredible sight meets your eyes! What once was a place of tattered hopes and broken-down dreams is now filled with the bright new beginnings of an exciting new you. The new mental furniture stands on the sturdy legs of self-assurance; you have replaced frustration and quiet resignation with the enthusiasm of promise and belief.

That is how positive thinking should work. That is the difference between just believing in positive thinking and actually creating it in your life. It is fine to throw out the old—it is essential. But it is also essential to replace the old with the new, word by word, thought by thought.

The problem has been that in the past, no one gave us the words. No one gave us the word-for-word vocabulary that we needed to replace the negative programming we had learned so well. The right kind of self-talk is the key to making all positive thinking work.

Just wanting to be a positive thinker isn't enough. Making the decision to have a positive attitude isn't enough. You have to wire the new habit into your brain. The human brain says: "Give me the directions, the commands, the picture, the schedule, and the results you want. Then I will do it for you. *Give me the words.*"

CHAPTER ELEVEN

Self-Talk and Motivation

The radio talk show host was saying, "My guest today is a motivational speaker and an author in the field of motivation." He concluded his introduction to the program by turning to me across the microphone and saying, "Shad, are you one of those guys who gets audiences jumping in the aisles and ready to run out and conquer the world?"

I think my answer surprised him. My response was, "No, I'm not. In fact, I really don't believe in motivation."

The next few moments may have been the first time there was that much dead silence on his radio show. He had been prepared to talk about the exciting world of motivation, and he had just realized that his guest was about to say it doesn't work.

But let me clarify. Some motivation works. It's just that most of it, maybe 95 percent of it, doesn't. I recall reading the comment from the training director of a large international corporation. He was interviewed by a national magazine, and the topic was on what is new in training—principally in the field of corporations and large organizations. He said that his company had decided to stop hiring speakers who were motivational without being instructional. A motivational talk, he had concluded, was much like the old saying about eating Chinese food for lunch; an hour later, you're hungry again. I don't know if that's really true about Chinese food, but it is true about motivation. Most motivation simply doesn't stick. It doesn't stay with you.

There are different kinds of motivation, and different kinds of motivators. One of the most popular kinds of motivation consists of an audience of listeners, sitting enthralled while a dynamically enthusiastic speaker weaves for them a web of pure magic, the spun gold of riches and success. For an hour or two he will imbue his listeners with a new sense of destiny, a grand new vision of their unlimited selves, all of them capable of scaling the highest mountains of their imagination, if only they believe that they can.

The members of the audience are given a new lease on life; the only payment required is that they begin the next day as the *new* person, conquering all odds, laying waste to their limitations, focusing on the goal and going for it. If you have ever attended a motivational talk such as I am describing, you know that I may be understating the magnitude of the mesmerizing that takes place.

Companies and groups of all sizes and descriptions rely on that kind of motivation to pep up their people, give a high point to their conventions and sales meetings, and send the troops away, ready to go out and fight dragons, close more sales, fix problems fast, and reach new heights of achievement.

Popular speakers, dynamic orators, enlightening the faithful with the contagious zeal of the greatest Sunday morning sermons, convince their listeners of their ultimate potential. And they do their best to do what they came there to do: *to motivate.*

These motivators do a good job of getting people thinking. They paint pictures, a gallery of suggested dreams, that show others what they *can* be, and what they can do. They paint the picture of success, leading the average would-be achiever toward something better. They stimulate minds, inspire new ideas, and reaffirm the resolve to get at it, get something done, accomplish something worthwhile, set some goals, tackle the problems, and move forward.

But there is a problem with that kind of motivation: No matter how good it is, *it is external, and it does not last.*

EXTERNAL TEMPORARY MOTIVATION

All *external* motivation is temporary. External motivation is the kind that may wake you up, but it will not keep you awake for long. External motivation is motivation that comes to you from the outside. It may influence you to make a change, but it cannot make the change for you. And it cannot keep you from drifting off course when the motivator is gone. It is the external coach who supports, encourages, demands, and rewards. But when the coach is gone, so are the support, the encouragement, the demand, and the reward.

Let's say that during the summer months, you play softball on a team that has the goal of winning the local tournament. Your team is fortunate to have an exceptional coach. He expects a lot from you, but he also gives you a lot of encouragement. He picks you up when you get down, helps you believe that you can win, and lets you know it when you've done a good job. He's a great motivator, and he takes your team all the way to the top. He is your friend, your ally, and your strongest supporter. You rely on him for your motivation, and you get it.

Then the season is over, and the coach goes home. What do you suppose he takes with him? Your motivation. *He* was your motivation. Now he is no longer around, and you have to get your motivation from somewhere else. Why? Because that motivation was external. It all came to you from the outside of you. And it was all *temporary* motivation.

All of our external motivation works the same way. Keep giving us the motivation, and we will do better. Take it away, and we will move, mentally, back to where we were before the motivation began. We may have progressed or grown or achieved something in the process, but we did so with someone else's energy; it was not our own.

That is why so many of the hopeful attendees at so many motivational talks get pumped up full of energy, ready to conquer the world, and then slow down or stop dead in their tracks weeks, days, or even hours after the speech is over. The inspiration they felt so strongly during the message is no longer there. The energy and enthusiasm that welled up inside of them is gone. The motivator left town. And so did most of the dream. All that often remains is enough left over to remind them of what they could have done, but didn't do.

That's because the convention hall or the banquet room was filled with individuals who, unless they had first learned how to do it differently, had brought their old mental programs with them. The motivators were talking to a room filled with old programs—programs that were designed to subconsciously reject the new information the motivator was trying to feed them! It takes more than an hour or two to override the old programming and replace it with the new.

It takes more than a rousing speech to erase and replace those internal programs that tell us we should know better than to suddenly believe that we are powerful champions of success. Lasting motivation takes more than the single reading of a book, getting an occasional talk from the supervisor or manager, or the encouragement of a friend.

The external motivation tells us that we can do anything we want to accomplish. Our poorly programmed internal motivator, our subconscious mind, says, *"Rubbish!"* We may believe the external motivator for a time—we *want* to believe it! But our longtime, comfortable old program patiently waits for us to come to our senses, believe what our past programming has taught us, and stop this nonsense about wanting to be a superachiever. Whether or not we are capable of achieving doesn't make a bit of difference to our subconscious minds. They are still acting on the tens of thousands of previous directions that told us "No you can't."

An hour or two of someone else telling us that "we can do it!" has too much old programming to overcome. The talk was inspiring. The ideas were incredible. But when the coach goes home—so does the motivation.

How much better it would be if that same inspiring speaker spoke to a crowded hall of *positive self-talkers*—people with new positive programs in their computers. A subconscious mind that has erased the old negatives and replaced them with new positives is the most fertile ground for growth and achievement we will ever find.

MANAGING OTHERS

Corporate executives and training directors should take note. If you have ever wondered why your own motivational programs must be repeated or reinforced so frequently, it is because it is physiologically impossible for momentary external motivation to create permanent change in the human brain. You can step up the amount of motivation and training you offer, increase its frequency, and never let the coach go home. But if the coach ever does leave, the old conditioning that is piloting your employees' ships will once again take over. Some of the external motivation may last a little longer than others, but all of it will eventually slow down and stop.

If you are responsible in any way for the training, development, motivation, inspiration, or direction of other people, regardless of your field—whether you are a business person, educator, clergyman, parent, or friend—remember that the people you are talking to *want to believe* in the best you are giving them. But always remember that their progress toward accepting, believing in, and acting upon it is first and always filtered through their own previous conditioning and programming.

If you truly want to reach them, work first with their self-talk. It is the unconscious self-talk they are using today that will determine whether they subconsciously open the door to you—or turn you away. Work first with the self-talk that's guiding them now, share with them the self-talk that will open the door, and then watch what happens. People want to improve, change for the better. Help them, with positive self-talk, see themselves in a different way, and they will.

There are, of course, many kinds of external motivation that look nothing like a motivational rally or pep talk. In fact, most of the motivation we receive is far less obvious. We rely on friends, books, family, luck, problems, achievements, and social pressures to tell us what to do and to keep us doing it.

One of our greatest daily motivators is the heap of demands of daily living. That is often what gets us up in the morning, gets us going, and motivates us to do most of what we do throughout the day. Most of us will admit that we feel we "have to," "should," "need to," or are "supposed to" do most of what we do. We have even found a popular word to express the result of too much of that kind of motivation: "stress." But these external motivators are also temporary. The motivation exists until the demands go away.

Most interesting, the human brain has no neural networks that are designed to store motivation—and the result is, the brain *doesn't* store it—it *can't*. Any motivation that comes to you from an outside source, no matter how exciting or powerful that motivation may feel at the moment, cannot be stored by your brain.

THE ONLY MOTIVATION THAT LASTS

Since, as I have found, the most accurate meaning of the word "motivation" is "to put into motion," it seems to me that when it comes right down to it, if a vote were taken, most of us would rather decide for ourselves what should put us "into motion" than to have someone else decide for us.

If you'd like to get motivated—and *stay* motivated—you have to have the right self-talk. The right self-talk creates *internal* motivation, which, because of the way the brain works, is the only kind of motivation that lasts.

The best solution to getting motivated and staying motivated is to practice being your own motivator.

Imagine having a coach who stayed with you, season after season and every day in between. Imagine not needing to wait for someone else to get you charged up and moving. Imagine being able to rely on yourself to always energize your spirit, focus your attention, and keep you in tune, on top, in touch, and going for it. Can you imagine never again needing someone else to prod or push you into activating your own best efforts?

Your own *internal coach* will do that, if you wire your brain with the right self-talk and tell it what to do. Your internal coach is your strongest believer. With the right self-talk and the right programming, that coach will show you the best in yourself and help you achieve it. It will give you direction, strengthen your will, and give you belief. It should become your ultimate motivator. It is *you.*

CHAPTER TWELVE

Not Hypnosis—Not Subliminal

I am often asked if self-talk is a form of hypnosis. In some ways, at first glance, self-talk might look like a form of self-hypnosis, but there are important differences between the two. Hypnosis takes temporary control of your receptive mind without the benefit of your conscious awareness. It is most frequently used to temporarily override unconscious programs in the brain. Self-talk, on the other hand, deals with a much broader range of mental programs and "permanently" rewires neural pathways in the brain through the use of conscious repetition.

Hypnosis requires the subject to enter a trance state, one of several levels of consciousness that open doors to the subconscious mind. In the field of psychology and in certain areas of medical science, there is still some disagreement about what, exactly, takes place when a person becomes hypnotized.

Most researchers agree that when individuals are placed in a hypnotic state, they are more receptive to certain kinds of suggestions. There also appears to be less "clutter" between the conscious mind and the unconscious mind—the distractions of the conscious mind are reduced and the individual is more open to subconscious suggestions and directions.

Some experienced practitioners in the field of hypnosis have concluded that hypnotic states are natural states of mind. So natural, in fact, that according to them, we are "hypnotically" influenced daily, by subtle subconscious suggestions of which we are not even aware.

As examples of its value, hypnosis has helped people reduce weight or stop smoking, and with others it has played a role in overcoming anxiety and fears. I have known people who found, with the aid of an experienced hypnotherapist, the source of and ultimately improvement in phobias or other problems they faced. In the medical field, hypnosis has proved to be effective in certain instances in the reduction or elimination of pain.

But the role of self-talk deals with a broader picture than these, and over a much longer duration of time. Self-talk and hypnosis differ not only in methodology, but also in philosophy. In most cases, with hypnosis, a hypnotherapist is responsible for temporarily overriding programs, or specific control centers, in your brain. With self-talk, you're in control, and instead of temporarily overriding programs, you're actually rewiring neural networks to create long-term changes to the structure of your brain itself.

So when an outside hypnotherapist is overriding your brain's programming with hypnotic suggestions that you're not consciously aware of, your progress is dependent on the qualifications of the therapist. But when you're fully aware of your own self-talk, and every program you're allowing to be wired into your brain, you're taking responsibility for yourself.

TAKING RESPONSIBILITY FOR YOURSELF

Personal responsibility is at the root of everything we think, do, conceive, fail at, or achieve in our lives. It is the bedrock of all individual action. Responsibility does not mean "duty" or "burden." It is not the measure of our liability or our accountability. It is the basis of our individual determination to respond to life and to fulfill ourselves within it.

The day you were born, there is a good chance there were a few other people around helping you into the world. Your mother was there, probably a doctor, and maybe a nurse or two. But no matter who patted you on the backside when you came struggling into human life, you took your first breath alone. No matter what help you may have received, *you* took that first breath by yourself. And the next breath, and the next. *You* did that. You may have had some help along the way, but the breaths you took were your own. No one breathed them for you.

One day, each of us will die. If you have ever stood at the bedside of someone who was passing out of this world, you know that no matter how tightly you might have held that loved one's hand, their last breath was breathed alone. When you or I take our last breath, in earthly matters, we will breathe it alone.

In spite of everything that anyone can do to help, in spite of the doctors and the assistants, in spite of the needs and tears of those who stay behind, when we leave, we will leave alone. There may be abundant spirits to guide us, but of those we leave on earth behind us, not one of them can share that journey with us. We take our first breath by ourselves, and we take our last breath by ourselves.

How, then, is it that somewhere in between, in that time we call *life,* we expect someone *else* to do our breathing *for* us?

No one will ever breathe one breath for us. No one will ever think one thought that is ours. No one will *ever* stand in our bodies, experience what happens to us, feel our fears, dream our dreams, or cry our tears. We are born, live, and leave this life *entirely* on our own. That "self," and the divine spirit that drives it, are what we have. No one else can ever live a single moment of our lives for us. That we must do for ourselves. *That* is *responsibility.*

Hypnosis is not intended to be a replacement for the responsibility each of us has to manage our own minds. It is, rather, a tool that may help us, at least temporarily, override some of the programs we have that are difficult to change quickly.

But practicing positive self-talk as a way of life plays a greater role than that. With active, daily self-talk, you, personally, are taking complete responsibility for yourself. You are consciously in control and in charge of the much broader scope of programs that affect every facet of your attitudes and your behavior.

SUBLIMINAL CONDITIONING

There is a near cousin of hypnosis that in past years has been popular from time to time. It is "subliminal" learning or conditioning, and in concept it works like this: While you're listening to a recording of sounds of an "ordinary" nature, such as soft music, the sound of rain, or a soothing forest stream, you are also being fed, unconsciously, messages that have been subliminally hidden within or under the other sounds.

An example of this would be a recording of specially selected music that also has imbedded into the soundtrack an inaudible spoken message. You hear the music, but you do not consciously hear the voice that is hidden under the music. It may be convincing you to stop smoking, reduce your stress, improve your relationship with your loved one, or make more money, depending on the subject that's being covered on the recording.

Although it has been around for years, subliminal messaging in audio recordings has not enjoyed the same popularity or respect as hypnosis, in most part because it appears to be a myth. I have concluded that in those instances where subliminal messaging may have appeared to have worked, it did so because the subject's belief in its working created a placebo effect. Any audio message that is recorded too quietly to hear it does not vibrate the ear drum, and no signal is sent to the brain.

Video subliminal imaging, on the other hand, may be another matter. Some of us remember stories from the 1950s and early 1960s when it was reported that movie theaters were inserting short subliminal messages into films to get us to rush out to the refreshment stand and buy a soft drink and some popcorn. The government got interested, theaters were cautioned to stop using subliminal advertising messages in films, and the furor over "mind control" died down and was, for the most part, forgotten. We learned later that the original stories themselves were not true, but the concept itself is still claimed to be valid.

Subliminal video images, added to movies or television programming, have the ability to create an emotional response from the viewer. This is somewhat different from subliminal audio messaging because the visual picture is actually viewed by the eye and the brain, but at such high speed that it's not consciously noticed.

A frame-by-frame viewing of some heart-pounding high-action movies, for instance, reveals split-second pictures of skulls and other gruesome images, carefully edited into the action sequences of the films. They go by so quickly at normal speed that the visual impression and its associated emotional triggers in our brains go almost completely unnoticed, yet the effect is very real.

Could subliminal techniques, placing hidden visual images on television, be used to convince us to use a certain brand of perfume or buy a certain beverage? I think that most advertising agency executives would privately vouch for the fact that they do. If the human mind is, as some have said, the playground of the powerful, those who would manipulate and control our thoughts must certainly be having a field day.

There are two key points here:

1. Self-talk is not hypnosis, and it is not subliminal. Self-talk gives *you* the power to program your own mind, *consciously,* every day, and it leaves the responsibility up to you.
2. There are those who would try to program *your* mind for *their* purposes. Take responsibility for the programming of your mind. By not taking responsibility for our own thoughts, we leave our minds open to the whims of others. As individuals, we should be capable of exerting more control over our own minds, individually, than any outside control or influence that anyone else would like to have over us.

I would encourage you to vote your own vote, think for yourself, and always be in control of what you are programming into your own subconscious mind.

Your self-talk, and the directions you give to your inner self, will always be your surest form of mental defense and inner strength. Combine that with your personal source of spiritual strength—and no one else can override it. Employ the resources of your mind. Call them to action. Think for yourself. Speak for yourself. Educate and program your own mind in the manner of your own choosing. No one else should do that for you. No one else has the right.

CHAPTER THIRTEEN

If It Isn't Simple, It Won't Work

The more we have learned about self-talk, the more ways we have found to use it—ways that make it easier to practice and learn and make it more lasting and effective at the same time.

No idea, no matter how good, will work if it doesn't get used. For many years, as I've studied the field of personal growth and examined the many concepts available, I have found concepts I liked a lot. They make a lot of sense, and should work. But many of them have been too difficult to put into practice, so either people don't try them, or after a short while, they stop using them.

Even with the most ardent self-improvement enthusiasts, any program that takes too much time, requires too much sacrifice, or is too complex to use easily will not get used. I suspect that some of the best self-improvement books and audio or video programs ever published are gathering dust on a shelf or are tucked away in some closet, safely out of sight and out of mind.

Some personal growth concepts too often fall into the same category as home-exercise machines that were used once and put away. They are like the barbells and gym sets or dance instruction videos that seemed like a good idea at the time we got them, but they took too much work. So we hid them away and told ourselves that we would bring them back out of hiding and get started using them a little later. Instead of having a revered place in the family den, and eventually being worn out through overuse, the books, gadgets, and costly gizmos of self-improvement often end up on the bargain tables of neighborhood garage sales.

I have met dozens of people who have told me about the personal growth programs they started, but never finished—let alone put into practice. I can sympathize with them. Wading through a personal growth program that demands a monastic regimen of diligence and self-sacrifice does not stimulate enthusiastic involvement. And even the simplest of programs can be hard enough to stick with.

When I first witnessed the sometimes astonishing effects that people were experiencing in their lives after putting into practice some of the personal growth ideas and techniques that they had learned, I was dismayed when I saw so many others failing to achieve the same things. I was saddened to see the results that low self-esteem and negative self-belief were creating in so many lives, when it was apparent that with a little effort on anyone's part, it did not have to be that way.

But I also observed how few people who wanted to make a significant change in their lives had the determination and self-motivation to *work* at making the change. It was only later, after I had analyzed the methods people were using to make the changes, that I understood why so few were using them. Unless an individual's predisposition to self-determination was strong enough—unless a person's heredity and early conditioning created an attitude and a will that *demanded* improvement and change—the normal obstacles of day-to-day life stopped them short.

Most of us know we could do better. I doubt that I could find ten people who would not say that they, too, would like to improve *something* about themselves. We are also aware of the benefits that creating improvements in ourselves creates in our lives.

We are well aware of the material advantages we would like to have—a new home or car, new clothes, furniture, more money in the bank, and anything we have set our hearts on that a little extra money could give us. Most of us would also like to have more time, more freedom to do the things we want—time to travel, time to spend with our families, time to relax, time to enjoy, time to create, or time to spend with others doing the things we most like to do. And many of us would like to improve our education, learn something new, take up new interests, and develop our skills.

THE COMPETITION OF DAILY LIVING

Through a natural law of cause and effect, when we improve ourselves, the things we would like to have in our lives follow naturally. Improve *who* you are, and by that same law, you will improve your life. The more successful you become inside, the more successes you will automatically create on the outside. But making changes on the inside is seldom as easily accomplished as we would like it to be.

When we want to improve ourselves in some way, we are not just competing with our old programming; we are competing with the requirements of daily living. Each of us has three resources that allow us to get through any given day. Those resources are our *time,* our *energy,* and our *mind* (what and how we think).

Our desire to improve ourselves competes with the time we

spend working, taking care of our families, and taking care of the rest of our needs. It competes with the energy we consume doing everything necessary just to keep our lives in some reasonable order. Sometimes, most days for some of us, there is just no energy left. Our desire to improve ourselves competes with the demands that we or others have placed on us mentally, as well. We have so many things to think about, so many small and big decisions to make, things to figure out, problems to solve, things to consider, understand, and deal with.

We are so busy taking care of first things first that we have no time, energy, or thought left to take care of the one thing that could make all of the other things work better. We are too busy fixing the train to realize that we are on the wrong track. We are too busy staying alive to figure out how to *live*.

I remember the excitement I first felt when, many years ago, as a young father going back to school, I happened upon what I thought to be the most exceptional self-improvement idea I had ever encountered. It was a simple idea, new at the time, that would require only that I spend twenty minutes each night writing my goals, reviewing my progress, and mentally visualizing reaching each goal I was setting. I didn't have to be convinced that if I spent even that small amount of time each day concentrating on my goals, especially at night just before I went to sleep dreaming about them, that I could achieve anything I wanted. It's still a great idea, one of the classics—and it can work.

What I did not know then, but soon learned, was that even twenty minutes a night is sometimes hard to come by. When you are, as I was at the time, holding down a job, raising a family, and also going to school with a full-time college-level course load, just trying to get five or six hours of sleep a night is a challenge. When my mind was somewhere between studying for a psychology exam and finishing a business plan that was due at eight o'clock the next morning at the office, the twenty minutes I was supposed to spend each night working out my goal plan and "improving myself" soon moved from an exalted position of importance to an impossible chore. It's hard to study your goals when you can't keep your eyes open.

That experience with self-improvement was not unique. The nightly goals idea itself might have been great, but, as I was to learn later, I was not mentally ready to make the idea work. I had not first wired my brain with the right mental tools to make the idea work.

THE RIGHT TOOLS

To this day, countless people have tried the same kinds of marvelous ideas, with the same results. Of those, too few of them stuck it out and stayed with it. I applaud those who have. But I feel deeply for those who have not, despite their desire to achieve their goals. *They just didn't have the right programs in place to get the job done.* They wanted to achieve, and if they had first rewired and replaced some of their programs, they would have.

How, then, can any good and true idea that clearly could improve our lot in life hope to succeed when few of us have the time, physical energy, or mental energy left over to even give it a try? The answer to that question is very important. It is the answer that will make one good idea work when another will not: *For any personal growth concept to be successful, it has to be simple. It has to be easy to use. It has to be easy to put into practice. And it has to work.*

CHAPTER FOURTEEN

The New Techniques

The techniques that make self-talk work so well are simple, and they are surprisingly easy to use. Some of the techniques require spending time using them, but some of the techniques require no time at all. There are five different methods for using self-talk; you may choose to use some or all of them:

SILENT SELF-TALK

This is the self-talk that goes on all of the time, although we are usually not aware of it. Silent self-talk can be either a conscious or an unconscious internal dialogue. When you begin to replace old negative self-talk with new positive self-talk, this is one of the easiest and most natural techniques to use.

Even now, after just becoming aware of the difference between the negative self-talk of Level 1 and Level 2, there is a good chance that you are already starting to use the positive self-talk of Level 3 and Level 4 when you silently talk to yourself. It is an easy change to make. It takes more awareness than effort, and soon becomes a natural and automatic self-talk habit.

Silent self-talk includes anything and everything you think

about yourself or anything else around you. It is that subtle shift in your attitude from ever again looking at things in a negative way to looking at everything in a more positive, productive way.

Instead of waking up in the morning and telling yourself you wish you didn't have to get out of bed, your new self-talk should tell you that it's a great day to be alive—and it's time to get at it. Since most of those things we call problems are really only *perceived* as problems, the way you look at each of them determines whether they really are or not; you need only tell yourself to see them in a better way. If you think that might sound a little too easy, try it for a day and see what happens.

Remember, when you begin rephrasing your self-talk from the old to the new, your old programming will try to talk you out of it. So when you get started, start first with the decision to not listen to the earlier negative program, which tries to tell you that it won't work. Remember, too, that your old self-talk is a habit. It feels natural and it feels comfortable, even if it is negative. By knowing what to expect, you will be ready to meet that old self-talk head on, override it, and begin building a new habit.

Within even a day or two, you will start to notice everything you have been saying to yourself that could work against you. When you have made the decision to throw the old furniture out of your mental apartment, you'll know when you are trying to bring it back in. Put your foot down. Get tough! Keep it out.

As you get started, during each day, listen to everything you say when you talk to yourself. Make a mental note of anything you think or say to yourself that sounds like the wrong kind of self-talk, and immediately turn it around and rephrase it in the positive. "I just can't seem to get organized today" immediately becomes "I am organized and in control, today especially!" When you hear yourself say something like "I've really got a problem with this . . ." turn it around and say, "I can handle this! I'm a capable person and I handle problems well." "I just can't seem to lose weight" becomes "Losing weight is never a problem for me. I eat exactly what I should and only the right healthy amount—I'm losing weight and looking great!"

Instead of telling yourself that you're tired—at a time of the day when you can't afford to be tired—*immediately* tell yourself that you have plenty of energy and enthusiasm. And if it doesn't suddenly make you jump up and down with energy, that's okay; you're working on a whole new way to talk to yourself, and you are starting to give your subconscious mind a new set of directions. Just keep doing it every chance you get, and it will start to work for you. How we "feel"—tired or energetic, listless or enthusiastic—is mental and *chemical;* it is physiological.

Think of a time when you feel like you don't want to even get up out of the chair. It has been a long day, you worked hard, and you are physically and mentally exhausted. Then the phone rings, and it is just the right phone call at just the right moment, someone calling with good news, or someone who is the most important person in the world to you. What suddenly happens to your energy? What happens to your enthusiasm? A surge of adrenaline hits your system and brings you back to life *instantly.*

Has anything really changed? Just the signals you sent to your brain, and, in turn, the switches your brain turned on for you, sending messages to every part of your system telling you to suddenly feel great, when only moments before you couldn't get out of the chair.

Many of the messages you give yourself through your silent self-talk may not be as obvious. But the brain responds just as immediately and produces results, whether they are noticed or not, that are just as powerful. Remember, the thoughts you think are electrical impulses that direct the brain to turn important switches in your mental control center on or off. By replacing your earlier negative or neutral self-talk with new commands, you are activating healthy, productive chemical and electrical control centers in your brain that will automatically work for you instead of against you.

We have all experienced times when one argument in the morning can ruin the whole day. Change the programming. Rephrase your silent thoughts to yourself. Instead of losing a day to depression or dejection, you will gain one more precious day of worthwhile accomplishment. You will feel better emotionally, you will be healthier, both mentally and physically, and you will get along better with others. Instead of chalking the day up as a loss, you will have earned yourself another win.

SELF-SPEAK

Anything you say out loud to yourself, or to someone else about yourself, or about anything else, is part of your self-talk. What you say when you are speaking makes up an important part of the pictures and directions you are feeding to your subconscious mind.

It makes sense that if what you say when you are speaking paints the wrong pictures or delivers commands that give yourself counterproductive information, the end result will be that your brain will act on the information in a way that could work against you in any number of ways. Telling a friend that you don't like your job cannot possibly help your job. You may make yourself feel better by getting it off your chest, and in most forms of therapy, that technique is used with some success. But how much better it would be if you were to change your attitude by changing the programming you were giving yourself, especially in those circumstances when the job (or any situation) isn't going to change just by complaining about it.

Your self-talk is at the heart of something we call "acceptance." There are times in life when all of us feel compelled to put up with a bad situation. But it is completely up to you whether you let that situation work against you, or make a mental decision to see it in a different way. Your self-speak and other forms of self-talk are the determining factors in whether the real you, the inside you, wins or loses.

The easiest way to determine which of the people around you are the real winners at life and which are not, is to listen to their self-speak—what they say when they talk about anything. Winners use self-speak to build an attitude that produces winning results. It doesn't mean that winners don't have problems. It doesn't mean that every day for them is a perfect day. But look at their average scores in winning at life, over a few months or a few years. The better their self-speak, the better their score. The more positive their approach, the more successful the results. In time, positive self-speak becomes as much an automatic habit as walking, moving, eating, or sleeping. And when positive self-speak becomes a habit, so do the successes that the self-speak creates.

Listen to everything you say when you speak. Do your words paint the picture you want your subconscious mind to see? If not, change the words. Rephrase them. Learning to build the best in yourself—by learning to give yourself a refreshing new program of self-speak—is one of the greatest gifts you will ever give to yourself. Once mastered, it is a treasure you will never lose.

SELF-CONVERSATION

This form of self-talk is one of the easiest to use, and it can also be a lot of fun. Self-conversation is the technique of actually talking to yourself *out loud* and holding down both ends of the conversation all by yourself! Self-conversation works because it engages more of your senses and puts more of you to work programming yourself in the new way. When you have a self-conversation, more of *you* gets involved!

For most people, practicing self-conversation may feel a little strange, but that's only because we weren't taught that talking to yourself was a good thing, especially talking to yourself out loud. (An exception to this is athletes who, increasingly, are trained to give themselves verbal motivation during an event.)

When you first begin to practice conversational self-talk, you may want to go into the bathroom and lock the door. When you start talking to yourself out loud, carrying on a conversation with yourself, asking yourself questions and answering them, even your most trusting family members may think you have finally gone over the edge.

On one occasion, I was flying from Chicago to San Francisco with a layover in Denver on the night of December twenty-third. Because of bad weather, our departure from Denver was delayed, and at twenty minutes after eleven P.M., we were informed that because of the snowstorm, we would have to spend several hours or possibly all night in the Denver airport.

Since it was the busy holiday season, all the planes were packed, and due to the planes being off-loaded at the Denver airport, the lobby and terminal buildings were rapidly filling up with passengers—none of whom were too happy about having to spend the night in the Denver airport, missing their connecting flights, and quite possibly not being able to make it home in time for Christmas Eve. I don't think I've ever seen so many irate people in one place at one time. Obviously they must have thought the snowstorm was the airline's fault—after all, who would blame God for making it snow the night before Christmas Eve?

After sizing up the situation, I decided this might be a good time for me to practice a little conversational self-talk. I wanted to get home just as much as anyone else, and I thought this would be a good time to test the effect of some instant programming. I looked around and noticed that the seats in the waiting area were filling up fast, and I noticed three seats side by side were still vacant. So I walked over, sat down in the middle of the three seats, and proceeded to talk to myself—out loud.

In a clear, confident, and loud voice I turned to myself "sitting" in the empty seat to one side of me and said, "Hi, Shad! Looks like we're grounded!"

"Yup!" I answered, just as confidently as I turned toward the empty seat on my other side. "What would you like to do?"

"Let's talk!"

Back and forth it went. And thus began one of the most interesting conversations I believe I have ever had—*with myself. It worked.* Not only was my stress level lower than anyone else's in that airport, but no one else sat down on either side of me all night!

There is, however, a less conspicuous and safer way to use self-conversation, and it is a way I recommend you try at your next available opportunity. I refer to it as shower talk, and it works like this: Tomorrow morning, when you step into the shower, say "Good morning!" to yourself. Say it out loud, and say it with a smile in your voice. Greet the day with your chin up, your attitude high, and tell yourself just how great the day ahead is going to be. "You look *great* today! You feel good, you're in good shape, and you're ready to tackle anything!"

And then respond—give yourself an answer back. "I feel *terrific!* Today especially! I feel good, I like who I am, and I'm glad to be alive and going for it!"

Even two or three minutes of that kind of rousing *internal* motivation can get you started on the right foot, facing the day, looking forward to it. It can get you moving and believing in a way that can change an average day into an exceptional day. And it *works*! Think how much better that kind of invigorating, positive-day-starting, confidence-building self-dialogue can be than the other ways we often use to start our day.

When I'm doing a training program for a corporation or for an organization, when I talk about getting yourself started in the morning with that kind of self-talk—self-*conversation*—of the most activating and vitalizing kind, I usually see in the audience a few people whose faces are registering what looks like something between amusement and incredulity. I must be kidding! But a few weeks later, after they have had a chance to try it awhile, I hear a different story. They try it, and it works.

Why *not* start your day with the absolute best about yourself? Why not come alive and tell yourself what you *can* do that day instead of groggily shaking your head over what you *cannot*? It has worked for business managers, salespeople, office workers, construction workers, athletes, students—anyone who wants to make today, tomorrow, and every day *count*.

Although you can carry on a self-conversation silently, you will find that when you talk to yourself out loud you are forcing yourself to put your thoughts into words. That helps you clarify your thinking on the subject and become much more specific than you are when you're just letting thoughts drift through your mind.

One of the benefits of talking to yourself in this way, out loud, and carrying on a conversation with yourself, is that this allows you to ask yourself questions and get straightforward answers. When you first try this, you might be surprised at the answers you get. We know ourselves pretty well—better than we sometimes think we do. The result is that most of the answers we get when we ask ourselves the right questions are the *real* answers—answers that get us to stop kidding ourselves and get down to the facts.

As I said, when you first begin to talk out loud to yourself, you might feel a little strange or foolish. I know I did. But in a day or two, the benefits will outweigh the minor embarrassment it might have taken to get started. In a short while, you will find yourself talking to yourself in the car, while you are alone in the office, while you're on a walk—anywhere at all.

Use a few of those precious moments of privacy we cherish so much. Tell yourself that you're okay—that you are *better* than okay. Go ahead, say it out loud! If you have a question you haven't found the answer to, ask it. *Take counsel with yourself.* You've got a pretty good friend in there who has been waiting to hear from you.

SELF-WRITE

Some people have told me that writing their own self-talk has been one of the most enjoyable projects they have ever embarked upon for themselves.

Other equally motivated would-be self-talkers have told me that *using* self-talk, reading self-talk, or listening to self-talk was great, but they simply couldn't find the time or perhaps the creativity within themselves to write, phrase for phrase, the self-talk they needed to achieve the changes they wanted to make.

Self-*write* is the kind of self-talk that you write out, word for word, for yourself. It is self-talk that is phrased in specific self-talk statements that deal directly with the most important new instructions you want to deliver to your subconscious mind—the new programming you want to work on most.

When I first explored finding practical ways to put self-talk to work, I began by writing out self-talk for each area of personal self-improvement, and then establishing a daily routine of reading the self-talk to myself. It had to be done every day to get the necessary repetition I needed to actually rewire my brain, and when I did it, it was effective. But it also took time and diligence. Other individuals who tried this method met with the same results, but in each case, the effectiveness was directly relative to the effort that the self-talker was willing to put into the project.

This early form of self-talk was written on index cards—one self-talk statement per card. Eventually, the persistent self-talk user would develop a card deck of self-talk phrases covering a variety of situations. Anytime a specific goal or problem came up, self-talk phrases from the card deck could be pulled out and used each day—again with repetition—until the goal was accomplished or the problem was under control.

Although the results were apparent, the effort it took to create the self-talk card deck often got in the way of successfully maintaining an ongoing do-it-yourself self-talk program. Eventually, after observing others who were working at using this technique, I came to the conclusion that most people simply are not conditioned to write self-talk. The result is that they don't.

In a number of my books I included self-talk phrases that others could follow and use to more easily write their own self-talk. I was well aware of the fact that a lot of people would rather do just about anything than have to sit down and write—especially something as detailed and precise as the specific wording and phrasing that is required to create the kind of self-talk that will reprogram the subconscious mind in just the right way.

That is not to say that writing self-talk has to be a chore. But unless you enjoy working with words and are willing to follow the "rules" of wording that work most effectively, no matter how much you wanted to begin using self-talk, you could get stopped almost as soon as you got started.

But for those who have learned what to write and how to state it, self-write is an effective way to reinforce the other tools you use to reprogram. It focuses your attention, makes you think, and gets you actively involved in the process of erasing the old negative programming and actively participating in the process of replacing the old with the new. That kind of focus—that amount of *involvement*—fine-tunes your initiative and adds energy to your determination.

Before you decide whether or not writing your own self-talk will be simple and easy for you, you should try it for yourself. If it doesn't work for you, there are other means to the end. If self-write *does* work for you, then you will not only enjoy the process—you will be delighted with the results.

RECORDED SELF-TALK

I first had the idea of listening to recorded self-talk in 1968. At that time, I was developing early versions of self-improvement tape programs for a sales company. I wrote and recorded one program in particular, which consisted of an early, somewhat primitive form of "I can do it!" self-talk as a motivational pep-talk cassette their salespeople could listen to when their sales were down. At that same time, I had also written a self-talk tape for myself that I had used to help me reach some of the professional and financial goals I had set for myself.

I suppose if I listened to those original cassette tapes now, I would be a little embarrassed about their distinctly nonprofessional quality. But they had met with some success; not only had a few of the salespeople profited by listening to them, but I, too, had profited just by listening now and then to some reassuring words of encouragement from rather inexpertly written and recorded home-brew cassette tapes.

Years later, in the 1980s, I would rekindle the idea when I was having trouble losing weight. Before trying self-talk to help me lose the weight I wanted to lose, I had tried just about everything else: diets that didn't work, weight-loss clinics that I didn't keep going to, self-created diet programs (usually called "starving yourself"), and combination programs that consisted of things like exercising for thirty minutes and then drinking nothing but grapefruit juice.

Somehow it always seemed that the more I exercised, the hungrier I got, and the more weight I took off, the more I felt I should reward myself with "a little something extra"—which usually amounted to something I shouldn't eat because it would put more pounds back on than the pounds I had just taken off. My story was just like the stories of tens of thousands of other weight-conscious dieters who took it off and put it right back on.

So I decided to try listening to self-talk to help me lose weight. When you want to fix a problem, you have to fix more than the symptoms—you have to give yourself a complete diet of self-talk covering every facet and every phase of your life that created the problem, or every area of your thinking that was tying you to the old mental programs. So I listened to self-talk that got behind the symptoms and into the causes, self-talk that would put me back in control, pep me up, and keep me at it.

The best part of it, other than the results I achieved, was that it didn't take any extra time or effort out of my busy day. It was easy enough to do; I simply changed that part of the soundtrack of my life by playing the new self-talk in the background. My brain, and the self-talk, took care of the rest.

Listening to self-talk worked, I lost the weight, and the success of doing that eventually led to the realization that anyone could benefit from listening to recorded self-talk for any area of their lives that needed help.

After more research on the subject, experimenting with exactly how the self-talk should be written and recorded, I would go on to record hundreds of self-talk sessions covering many areas of life, from health and fitness to relationships, self-esteem, career, finances, stress, and even self-talk sessions for children.

In time, I wrote and produced special sets of recorded self-talk cassettes on many topics. During the 1980s, I was fortunate enough to have those self-talk programs featured on popular nationally televised infomercials. (One was called *Sixty Minutes to Success,* another one was called, naturally enough, *Self-Talk for Weight-Loss,* and another one was *Self-Talk for Kids*.) With those television programs airing endlessly, along with my being invited to make repeat appearances on *The Oprah Winfrey Show* and CNN, soon self-talk was being listened to by thousands of people, and the results were coming in. Self-talk was working—and it was changing lives.

What's interesting is that the people who were watching the television programs and ordering the sets of recorded self-talk cassettes often didn't know anything about self-talk or programming or rewiring neural pathways in their brain—they were just ordering the self-talk, listening to it, and it was working. More and more individuals began to recognize the incredible importance of reprogramming the subconscious mind, and the natural capability of something as simple as listening to the right self-talk to help them get the job done.

With the advent of recorded self-talk, finally there was a method—a *technology,* based on science, that combined solid programming principles with a tool that anyone could use, and yet that would work as well as or better than any of the other techniques that existed prior to that time. In addition, it was a technological tool that functioned in the same way that the brain actually works.

Since that time, recorded self-talk on many subjects has been listened to by countless individuals, and it keeps working in marvelous ways. Not long ago I was giving a seminar on self-talk to a large audience. During a break, while I was signing books and talking to people who had come up to the podium to say hello, a family came up to talk to me. The family consisted of an elderly gentleman, a middle-aged husband and wife, and a boy about six years old.

The older gentleman introduced himself, and then went on to tell me that he had attended a self-talk seminar I had conducted twenty-five years earlier, and he had brought his young son with him to that seminar. At that time, he had taken a set of self-talk cassettes home with him. He had played the self-talk daily, and it had made many positive changes in his life. While he was listening each day, his son was also listening, and he, too, was flourishing, doing great at home and at school.

The man then proudly told me that the middle-aged man standing next to him now was his son, and the young boy with them was his grandchild—and to that day, they were, still, all listening to self-talk. Standing in front of me were *three generations* of positive self-talkers. And they were remarkable: bright, smiling, alert, positive, going-for-it individuals, who had made self-talk a part of their lives. The six-year-old grandson, smiling as he stood in front of me, had understood everything I had said about self-talk in my seminar. He, like his father and his grandfather, had *lived* it. And the light was in his eyes.

I had heard countless self-talk success stories from countless individuals over the years. But to me, that moment, perhaps beyond any other, not only lifted my spirits to the sky, it proved to me that my own dream had come true. Lives were changing, *generations* were changing, because of self-talk.

WHETHER BELIEVING OR NOT

A typical example of the stories I'm told is found in a letter I received from a woman who, after attending a seminar on self-talk, had decided to listen to recorded self-talk to help her with her "family relationships"—in particular, her relationship with her husband. Things hadn't been going too well for them, financially or otherwise, and she wanted to put things straight. Meanwhile, her husband was showing all the signs of making a slow but predictable departure from the relationship.

The woman had graduated from writing self-talk cards and reading them to herself, to listening to recorded self-talk. She listened to a session on improving personal relationships, a session on self-esteem, a session on goal-setting, and another session on taking responsibility for yourself. She listened to self-talk each morning, when she could during the day, and each night just before she went to sleep. To listen to the self-talk, she let the sessions play aloud, but in the background. According to her, when she first began playing the positive self-talk in the background, her husband could not have cared less.

But after a week or two, her husband took her to dinner one evening, and during dinner they discussed the self-talk she was listening to. He still showed every sign of disinterest in the self-talk the next day, but as she had learned in the seminar, "Don't worry too much about what the other people around you think about your self-talk. Just keep doing it."

By the end of the third week, her husband asked her to replay one of the sessions she had been playing while they were getting dressed one morning. Earlier, she had noticed that they were arguing less, but until that morning, he had never shown any active interest in the self-talk she was listening to each day. Shortly thereafter, the husband began to exhibit noticeable changes in his behavior toward her and in his attitude about the problems he had been having on his job.

The end result was that *both* of them began to talk more, started making some new plans, and started working together again. *Her* self-talk had the same effect on him as it did on her! It made no difference whether he believed in the self-talk or not. *His subconscious mind didn't care;* it simply acted on the new information he was unconsciously programming. He was, without even thinking about it, accepting the new, more positive programming that was being played as a background to their daily lives. Initially, one of them "believed," and the other did not. It didn't make any difference.

In your own practice of self-talk, the most immediately helpful thing you can do is to listen to self-talk. Many people start with listening to the self-talk sessions that are designed to help them reach their goals. That's because the area of goal-setting and goal achievement is where the external results of the internal changes you're making are lived out in every moment of your day, and you can see the first results almost immediately. Since self-talk sessions can now be streamed directly to your smartphone or any listening device, listening in this way has become very popular, and it's also practical.

Listening to recorded self-talk sessions has some advantages going for it that are as yet unrivaled in the self-development field. The first and most important advantage is that you can listen to positive self-talk that is wiring your brain and improving your life while you're doing something else. You don't have to focus on listening. Because the self-talk is being played loud enough to be heard, and it's clearly audible, even if it's playing softly in the background, your subconscious mind will be listening, and it will be busily programming the new positive information about you whether you're consciously thinking about it or not.

Another advantage to listening is that doing so with today's technological advantages is especially convenient—so it's a tool you actually end up using. All you have to do is tap on the menu of self-talk sessions listed on the screen of your smartphone, select the subject you want to listen to that day, and start listening. Everyone who does this soon learns that it is a lot easier than writing out scripts of self-belief, reading and rereading a book, or trying to study a course in self-achievement.

Yet another important advantage is that the recorded sessions, because they are available anytime we want to listen or anytime we need their help, give us a "coach" that uses the right self-talk to give us immediate external motivation when we need it most. At the same time, it programs our subconscious minds with a winning script of *internal* motivation to give us lasting results.

One of my favorite self-talk sessions is titled "Believing in Incredible You." It is impossible to listen to that session without feeling better, thinking better, *doing* better, within the first few minutes of listening. And while it is gearing me up and getting me going, filling me with the kind of enthusiasm that turns an average day into an exceptional day, it is also carefully and busily reprogramming me to make *every* day more effective, more productive, more self-fulfilling in every way.

Listening to that kind of self-talk session is like having a personal coach, a best friend, standing at your side, encouraging, motivating, uplifting, believing, and pushing you forward *that day, that moment,* helping you extract and achieve the best from yourself.

If you would like to avail yourself of one of the most worthwhile methods of setting up your own future to the good, I encourage you to listen to self-talk. Of all the ways to practice self-talk, listening to the right self-talk is the most immediately helpful and the most enduring. Just tap the screen, go about your day, and let it play. Your subconscious mind will be listening.

CHAPTER FIFTEEN

Getting Started

Now let's review what we've learned about self-talk, and how you can best get started using it.

Since I first started researching and writing about self-talk in the 1980s, we've learned a great deal about it, and how to change it. Today, people all over the world have become "positive self-talkers," and the interest in self-talk continues to grow dramatically. While the inaugural edition of this book was first published in 1986, its readership never stopped expanding, and today, editions are published in over seventy countries, and that number is still growing.

As the popularity of self-talk has grown, there has been an increasing torrent of people who want to change their programs and rewire their brains by practicing positive self-talk. As we just saw, recorded self-talk sessions with specially worded, repeated self-talk phrases have been listened to in every format from early cassette tapes to compact discs to today's self-talk sessions that are now streamed on the Internet. People read self-talk from daily inspirational calendar books in the series titled *365 Days of Positive Self-Talk* that I began publishing in 2015, and thousands of followers have read my self-talk posts each day on Facebook.

The reason positive self-talk has grown globally in popularity is due to research in the field of neuroscience that has shown the major role self-talk plays, *scientifically,* in our attitudes, our health, our well-being, and in our success throughout our entire lives. And people *get* it. In our computer-driven age, people quickly understand the basics of self-talk and programming, and they want to know how to use the science of self-talk to make their own lives better.

Fortunately, we've learned very specifically how to do that. There is a three-step process that I've taught in recent years that nails the job of making self-talk work. The key steps are *Monitor*, *Edit*, and *Listen*. Here it is:

MONITOR

Monitor your self-talk. Practice being aware of all of your words and thoughts.

The best way to monitor your self-talk is to practice *mindfulness*. As we're using it here, mindfulness is "being aware of being aware." The concept comes to us from the practice of meditation, and it has proved to be a major player in the science of well-being. Mindfulness not only helps you become aware of what you're thinking at all times, it also creates balance, reduces stress, and lowers the volume of the amygdala—the brain's fight or flight alarm system.

The reason mindfulness is so important to self-talk is that in order to change it, you have to start by being aware of what your self-talk is now, and you can do this by creating the habit of monitoring your self-talk at all times. Listen for any message you give to yourself that could wire your brain to work against you. Listen to both the words you say out loud and the words you say silently, or think, to yourself. (Self-talk is going on in our brains all of the time, although we're aware of less than 10 percent of it.) Your self-talk can be either a conscious or an unconscious dialogue, and it includes everything you think about yourself or anything else.

When you start monitoring your self-talk, you'll be listening carefully to yourself, so you'll start to notice things you've been saying to yourself that could be working against you. When you're aware of the self-talk you're using now, you'll know what you want to change.

EDIT

When you hear yourself using the wrong kind of self-talk, either thinking or saying the wrong thing, *immediately edit the message.* Change it. In that moment, turn it around and rephrase it in the positive. "I just can't seem to get organized today" immediately becomes "I am organized and in control, today especially." When you hear yourself say something like "I've really got a problem with this," turn it around and say "I can handle this. I'm a capable person and I handle problems well." In addition, "I just can't seem to lose weight" becomes "Losing weight is not a problem for me. I eat exactly what I should and only the right healthy amount—I'm losing weight and looking great."

We make hundreds of comments or statements on any given day. It might not seem important to phrase each of those messages in a positive way. But consider that each of those messages is actually a directive to your subconscious mind, and those that are repeated often enough will be physically wired into your brain. Then add up those thoughts and comments over a *year*. They add up to tens of thousands of very important subconscious self-directives. They're important—and they have a great deal to do with what you accomplish, how you feel about anything, and who you become.

By itself, editing your self-talk won't erase the old programs you already have. But if you keep doing it, editing will forever stop you from wiring in any more of the same.

LISTEN

As we learned in the previous chapter, many people who want to change their self-talk listen to sessions of positive self-talk phrases that are downloaded or streamed to their phones or tablets.

They do this because learning new self-talk is very much like learning a new language. You learned your first language by having it spoken around you—in the "background" of your life. When you were first learning the language you grew up with, your brain recorded the words and phrases you were hearing each day, and with repetition, wired them in permanently. Wiring your brain now, by listening to repeated self-talk phrases, works exactly the same way.

As I mentioned, when I was first researching the subject of self-talk, I had a personal breakthrough. I wanted to lose weight, and to help me do that I decided to listen to specially worded self-talk recordings that I played in the background for about fifteen minutes each morning while I was shaving. By listening to the repeated self-talk phrases in this way each day, I was rewiring my brain to see myself in a slimmer, healthier new way. It worked, and it changed my life. In the next ten and a half weeks, I lost fifty-eight pounds, shaving!

To this day, the weight has never come back. I got rid of

the old programs that had caused the weight problem in the first place. After all the struggle, after I tried so many other approaches only to face one disappointment after another, I finally found a solution that lasted. I got the positive results I had wanted all along—by listening to the right self-talk, I rewired my brain.

THE KEY IS REPETITION

It was the experience of using new positive self-talk to lose weight that first made me aware that anyone who wanted to change their self-talk, no matter what they wanted to improve in their life, could do so by listening to repeated self-talk each day, as I had. The result of that experience was that now people all over the world listen to self-talk every day.

Listening to self-talk is the most effective means I've ever found for changing our programs. After years of seeing so many people change their lives by listening, I have come to the conclusion that self-talk should be listened to in *every* home, *everywhere* (and I've been working on that). It would change the world.

The reason listening to self-talk is so effective is that it gives you the *repetition* that is required to rewire your brain. And it does so without your having to take any extra time, or consciously work at it. As we've seen, the more often the same messages are repeated, the stronger the brain wires them in. Listening to self-talk each day while you're getting ready in the morning, driving the car, going about your day, or listening when you're going to sleep at night, creates that repetition.

Note: To view the list of available self-talk sessions, or to stream self-talk sessions to your listening device, go to: www.shadhelmstetter.com.

CHAPTER SIXTEEN

Whatever Your Need or Position in Life

When you begin to actively practice self-talk, what you first use it for will depend on what you want to fix first or achieve first. But since self-talk becomes a self-generating habit—*the more you use it, the more you use it*—its success will depend more on getting started than on what you decide to use it for first.

It makes no difference what you do for a living, what your educational background is, what your problems may be, or what your goals are. It doesn't matter whether you have succeeded or failed in the past; the workings of the human brain are completely indifferent to your situation in life. Anyone can use self-talk and benefit from its results.

To give you just a few examples of the many ways in which the use of active self-talk can make a difference, let's look at some of the circumstances in our lives that can be helped or improved with the kind of self-talk we're discussing. The possibilities for using self-talk are limited only by the individual; there are as many uses as there are people with needs. Most of these examples, at some time and in some way, apply to all of us.

If you want to conquer a problem or overcome an obstacle:

Changing your self-talk can fix many kinds of problems. The problem can be anything you want to conquer—large or small. You may want to use self-talk to change attitudes or actions—or choices you make repeatedly that cause you problems. Sometimes even a small amount of exactly the right self-talk will help you take a minor step that creates major results. If you have a problem of any kind, ask yourself the questions, "Is my old self-talk contributing to this problem? Could changing my self-talk help me fix it?"

If you want to reach goals:

Practicing self-talk while you're setting good goals is one of the most important means to achieving them that I have ever found. Setting goals, and working at reaching them, is part and parcel to becoming healthy, wealthy, and wise; worthy goals are essential to true and lasting self-fulfillment.

Imagine setting worthwhile goals—and then fueling them with the nonstop energy of self-talk. You could achieve them without it, perhaps, but the road would be harder. Give life to your dreams, give strength to your visions, and give light to your path. Grant your journey the assurance of a safe arrival. Set your goals, work at achieving them, and talk to yourself every day along the way.

Setting goals and positive self-talk go hand in hand. But talk to yourself in exactly the right way, and you will find the road easier to follow. If you are not yet setting goals—and writing them down—you should. If you are already an active goal-setter, give to your goals the gift of your own self-assurance. Add the words of daily direction and encouragement of self-talk to your goals. Any well-set goal deserves the benefit of well-said words.

If you want to improve your job:

In one way or another, we are all subject to the directions of others. We all have rules that we have to follow. How you view your job, your vocation, your associates, and your employer, boss, or supervisor will have an important effect on how well you do and how you feel about yourself in the job you are in. If you tell yourself that you do not like your job—you probably won't. If you tell yourself that you are unhappy with your manager or employer, you probably will be.

Give yourself an advantage. Talk to yourself about your work and the people you work with in a way that makes your work *work* for you.

If you ever find yourself falling into the habit of finding fault with, complaining about, criticizing, or resenting your job, step aside and talk to yourself. There are others who have it far worse; some of them would love to have the opportunity that you now have. Your job, or your occupation, does a lot more than pay the bills. It gives you the opportunity to excel, to expect the best of yourself and to put that expectation into practice. Your success will always depend on what you think, what you tell yourself most. Expect the best, and then tell yourself the best. If you do, there is a good chance that is what you will get.

If you are in management:

There are two parts to good management. Effective leading of others always begins with successful self-management. You can be a graduate student of human resources or management and never attain the essential skills for managing others if you do not first master the management of yourself. True leaders have their own selves firmly in control; they are in command of their actions, their feelings, their attitudes, and their perspectives.

The second essential ingredient of being a good manager is knowing how to develop the qualities and skills of others.

Both of these management requirements are directly affected by self-talk. If there are two equally qualified managers, similar in every respect, and one of them uses positive self-talk with himself or herself, and the other does not, and the same manager develops positive self-talk attitudes in his or her employees, and the other does not, which manager has the better chance of succeeding and which does not?

Managers have an exceptional opportunity to apply self-talk to nearly every situation they encounter, every business day. If you want your business to compete, grow, and prosper, put self-talk to work with your management team. Instead of replacing people, start replacing their internal "cannots" with capable, confident self-belief. Self-talk does that. And one of the areas it does it best is in managing others to get the right job done in the right way.

If you want to earn more income or improve your financial strength:

Our earning potential is individually determined by each of us. The limits of our income are set by our own internal beliefs. If you want to earn more, you have to start by seeing yourself as worthy, deserving, and capable.

Too many of us, when we want to increase our earnings, make the mistake of tackling the problem from the wrong end. We try to figure out how we can earn more money before we believe we are capable of doing it. Talk to yourself about your self-worth. When you start to create a new picture of yourself being worth more, your subconscious mind will help you find a way to go about earning it. I don't want to oversimplify the task of making a significant increase in your financial net worth, but I have learned that doing so is far more dependent upon attitude, belief, and determination than on the position you are presently in today.

If you are serious about wanting to increase your income, begin by giving yourself three weeks of self-talk for self-worth and financial worth—*then* set your goals and write your plan. When you determine who you really are *inside,* and what you are really capable of accomplishing, it is much easier to see what to do next. Start with your programming; the rest will follow.

If you raise children, teach them, or work with them in any way:

A frequent story I hear is that of how the introduction of new self-talk in a home has affected the children. In most instances, it is one or both of the parents who begin using positive self-talk to work on some problem or to help them reach some of their goals. Since the use of self-talk in one area usually spreads to giving yourself the right kind of self-talk in other areas, it is not surprising that children, when they hear it used repeatedly in the home, begin to pick it up and use it almost accidentally.

It has always struck me how children accept positive self-talk *naturally,* even more easily than some of their parents. It may be that children are more willing to enthusiastically welcome anything that tells them *good* things about themselves. Children are closer to the original potential we were born with. Until we became programmed to believe what we could not do, we, when children, were still willing to believe in what we could. Our inner selves would far rather hear the best of who we can be than hear a daily discourse on the mistakes we make.

Imagine a home in which one of two children was allowed and encouraged to listen to and learn positive self-talk, while the second child was not allowed to learn self-talk or benefit from it. If those two children were similar in other respects, imagine how each of them might respond differently to situations in their young lives.

What children think about themselves will affect how well they do in school, the kind of friends they choose, how well they get along with others, how they deal with the problems of teenage expectations, how they keep themselves in control when peer group pressure encourages them to take the wrong path, the kind of mate they will eventually choose, the kind of career they'll follow, and how well they will do in every big and small area of their lives.

If there were two such children, one whose self-talk created strong self-esteem, good habits, and a positive "Yes I can" spirit, and one who was left to rely on the average unsure programming most children receive, which one would you vote for? I would vote for the child with the winning self-belief. Along with the inborn characteristics handed down by heredity, the self-belief *is* the child. Children *will become* what they believe about themselves most.

Parents have asked me why their son or daughter has chosen the worst possible kind of friends to associate with. All of us, and perhaps teenagers especially, seek out others whom we unconsciously believe we are most like. If a child has a less than positive picture of himself or herself, he or she will select those friends who are most like that picture—even if those friends are the wrong kind of friends. Give children a better self-image, a better self-picture, and they will choose more of their friends from the group that fits the same kind of picture. If a teenager is told he's no good, and believes it, he'll find others who are just as no good, or worse.

Self-talk can change that. Because self-talk changes the picture—*it changes the programming, which creates the belief, which develops the attitude, which creates the feelings, which controls the behavior.* If you'd like your child to do the *right* things, start at the beginning. Start with his or her self-talk.

If you'd like to do better in school—or anytime you are improving your skills:

You may not be in school at the moment, but if you are, or if you ever plan to go back, your self-talk could be the deciding factor in how well you do in school—academically and personally. First off, self-talk can help you with the basics; it can help you listen better, have more concentration, develop and keep good study habits, improve your determination to stay with it, sharpen your memory, and keep your spirits up and your eye firmly fixed on the goal ahead.

Doing well in school or at learning anything is no different than achieving in any other part of life; the exact same attitudes, skills, and self-belief are required. But studying and learning do impose special demands that require special kinds of self-talk. There is no doubt that the program that operates your internal computer will have a direct effect on your scholastic success. If you could use some help, either in school or out, make sure your own computer has the program that is getting you where you want to go. Add self-talk to your curriculum. You'll get more from school and more from yourself.

If you ever get down, feel lonely, or become depressed:

If things aren't going so well, it's time to change the program and start things looking up again. Using self-talk to deal with loneliness or depression is one of its best uses and one of the easiest to put into practice. Because self-talk deals with you and what you think, it deals directly with the root of the problem. In the case of loneliness, it is more than self-talk's self-conversation that can help. It is true that some of the time you spend alone may be best spent engaged in a worthwhile conversation with yourself. But it is the reprogramming that the self-talk conversation creates that is most helpful in turning the experience of being alone into an experience that is positive and profitable.

Fortunately, almost anything that we create in our lives, we can also change. But changing it has been the hard part. The despair and despondency of depression are all too often a part of many of our lives. But those kinds of depression that are self-created *can* be lightened or removed; the thoughts and the mood that caused them in the first place can be replaced—by the refreshing change of mental scenery that self-talk creates.

Any of us can talk ourselves *into* depression and discouragement—and we can as easily talk ourselves *out* of it. It doesn't take an iron will or a special formula; it takes a new word-for-word program that will redirect our self-belief, an adjustment in our pictures of ourselves and what's going on around us.

It is our choice to see things any way we want to see them. If we want to view our circumstances as dark and discouraging, we can. If we would rather view our circumstances as acceptable, hopeful, changeable, and positively possible, we can. But it takes more than just *wanting* things to work out right. That's why things didn't work out right in the first place—we hadn't given ourselves the right pictures, the right input to create the right output. And that's something any of us can do something about.

When dealing with depression, counselors often recommend the right diet and the right physical activities to help counteract the depression. I would add to that recommendation a healthy diet of new positive self-talk, and the daily activity of putting it to work.

If you would like to achieve:

Each of us, everyone you or I could ever meet, would like to achieve *something*. For some of us, it is to become better at something or achieve in only one or two areas of our lives. For others, it is to achieve the best we can in every area. If you were to make a list of those parts of your life, those problems, circumstances, or opportunities that self-talk could help you overcome, deal with, or attain, the list could be almost endless.

If you want to develop better self-esteem, get more done, change jobs, learn a new skill, become more creative, reduce stress, take better care of yourself, stop worrying, overcome depression, break through your limitations, get along better with others, or become more successful at anything, your own self-programmed self-talk lies at the root of your success.

Think of any job, career, position, task, or opportunity that comes to your mind. In any circumstance we might encounter, which of us has the better chance of succeeding, those of us who have given ourselves the extra benefit of self-assurance and determination, or those of us who hang on to our old programming and live with uncertainty, doubt, and disbelief?

Which would you rather do? Imagine for a moment any problem you would like to overcome, right now, or any change you would like to make in yourself or in your life. If there were two of you, and one of you became a positive, productive self-talker, and the other did not, for whom would you cast your vote? I know which one I would vote for, every time.

CHAPTER SEVENTEEN

Changing Habits

Of the many ways you can use self-talk in its various forms, you will find that all self-talk suggestions or phrases fit into one of four categories: *habit-changing, attitude building, motivational,* or *situational* self-talk.

Most of us have a habit or two that we would like to change. It is usually something we do that causes us problems (or causes other people problems). These are the habits that get in our way, hold us back, or in some cases, stop us completely—they are the well-trodden paths that, even though they lead us in the wrong direction, we most easily follow.

All habits are the result of our previous conditioning—things we learned to do, and practiced them until they became what seems like a natural way to behave. They are not natural at all, of course; we weren't born with any of them. They are habits—negative programs that stuck. Any of them can be replaced with a new program.

Habit-changing self-talk helps you work on a specific problem. This is the self-talk that directs your subconscious mind to stop doing something one way and start doing it another. It is the self-talk that replaces a behavior pattern that works against you with a behavior pattern that helps you solve problems or reach goals by changing your actions. Let's look at a few of the more common habits with which all of us are familiar.

- Putting Things Off or Procrastinating
- Working Too Hard or Not Working Hard Enough
- Arguing
- Ignoring Problems
- Oversleeping
- Smoking
- Forgetting Names or Other Important Things
- Being a Complainer
- Making Excuses
- Losing Things
- Overindulging—Eating or Drinking Too Much
- Being Sarcastic
- Saying "Yes" When You Want to Say "No"
- Never Being On Time
- Not Listening
- Blaming Others
- Interrupting Other People When They're Talking
- Being Disorganized
- Not Telling the Truth
- Worrying
- Being a Gossip
- Not Setting Priorities
- Letting Your Emotions Control You
- Wasting Time
- Giving Advice That Isn't Asked For
- Spending More Money Than You Earn
- Talking Too Much

- Being Overly Critical of Others
- Not Taking Care of Details
- Starting Something but Not Finishing It

All of these are habits, and all of them can be changed or improved upon with the right kind of self-talk.

Whether a habit you would like to change is as simple as interrupting others, or getting something done on time, there is a specific kind of self-talk that will help you do just that. Habit-changing self-talk is specific and demanding. It refuses to tolerate or accept the *old* habit while it creates a new picture of you acting and behaving in a way that puts the old habit behind you; it puts you into motion with a productive new habit pattern that replaces the old.

PUT YOUR SELF-TALK IN THE PRESENT TENSE

All positive self-talk, with the exception of situational self-talk, is written, read, recorded, listened to, thought, and spoken in the *present tense.* It is always stated as though the desired change *has already taken place.* By doing this, you are giving your subconscious mind a completed picture of the accomplished task; you are presenting your control center with the command that says, "This is what I choose. This is the 'me' I want you to create for me." The more finished or complete the picture, the more specific the directions you are giving your subconscious mind will be.

When you want to give a new directive to your subconscious you would not say, as an example, "I'm going to lose weight." When you say, "I'm going to . . . ," what are you actually telling your control center? "Tomorrow, later, some other time, I'll lose weight in the future ('I'm going to'), but for now, keep me like I am." And tomorrow never comes.

If you tell yourself, "I will, I'm going to, I need to, I should, I'd like to, I want to," or "I wish I could," I don't doubt that your subconscious will believe you: It just won't do anything about it!

State your goal or the result you want to achieve in the present tense. Because the subconscious mind does not know what is true and what is not, in time it will accept what you are telling it and act on it. But remember, it will attempt to follow the *exact* wording of the directions you are giving it.

I always do everything I need to do, when I need to do it.

I never argue or let my emotions work against me.

I don't smoke.

I have a good memory. I easily and automatically remember any name or anything that is important to me.

I eat only what I should.

I am a good listener. I hear everything that is said. I am attentive, interested, and aware of everything that is going on around me.

I have the courage to state my opinions. I take responsibility for myself and everything I say and do.

I never spend more than I earn. I am financially responsible, both for my present and for my future.

I set goals and I follow them. I set my sights, take the appropriate action, and achieve my goals.

I spend time with my family and my loved ones. I enjoy sharing their lives with mine and my life with theirs.

Each of these examples of positive self-talk deals directly with "habits"—conditioned styles of behavior that frustrate us or hold us back. In each case, the examples state the change in the present tense, as though the desired result has already taken place, but each example states only a single self-talk phrase or two out of many that, in actual practice, you would use to create the change you want to make.

When you are using self-talk to change a habit, affect an attitude, or create internal motivation, it works most effectively when you build a solid body of self-talk around the subject you are working on. One phrase of the right kind of self-talk can have an effect on your behavior, but it is only when you paint *an entirely new picture* for your subconscious mind that you will derive the full benefit from your self-talk.

If you were to choose one of the examples we just used, and wanted to change an old habit by using just *one* self-talk phrase only, no matter how often you repeated that bit of self-talk, it would have only limited results. Instead, start with that one phrase and extend it, add to it, and cover every part of the problem by including self-talk phrases that cover every hidden corner.

Remember, your new self-talk is the navigation system you're using to chart your new destination and determine your course, direction, altitude, and speed. So be specific and be thorough. Don't expect vague directions, hints of solutions, and shadows of expectations to get you where you're going.

BE SPECIFIC

When you use self-talk, leave no stone unturned. Isolate the problem, look at it from every angle, make a list of every area *within that problem,* and add a line of self-talk to cover it. While I have found few problems that can be solved with a single phrase or two of self-talk, I have found that in most cases any specific problem or goal can be covered with as few as a dozen or so well-worded self-talk phrases.

Let's look at an example of self-talk for changing habits. In this instance we'll use self-talk to tackle a habit that holds a lot of people back from reaching their full potential—the habit of wasting time on worry. Conquering just this one negative habit has turned underachievers into winners and given them extra time, peace of mind, and a fresh new outlook on life.

Once again, when you read the examples of habit-changing self-talk, notice that the self-talk doesn't just talk about the symptoms—it breaks the old habit down and gets at its roots. The new positive self-talk covers the problem from every angle. You should, by reading these few phrases of self-talk, very quickly recognize that the difference it can make is not one that will occur by using just a simple phrase or two.

Self-talk is at its strongest and most effective when it is composed of *a specific set of concisely worded directions—usually a group of a dozen or more combined phrases, linked together on the same subject, that jointly paint a detailed picture of the better you that you would like to become, or the change in your life you would like to create.*

In this example the old habit has been supported with daily negative self-talk—the kind we talked about earlier: "No matter what I do, I'm stressed out all the time," "I just can't relax," or "The problems in my life never stop; I can't get a break!" That's the old programming. But the new *habit-changing* self-talk looks at all of those things differently.

In the following self-talk, watch every phrase for the picture it presents; note the instructions that are being given, word for word, to the subconscious mind of the individual who used to think that stress and worry were destined to be a permanent problem.

This is the k[illegible] pletely new, be[illegible] shows you a na[illegible]ally *being* the worry-free, mo[illegible]d like to become.

POSITIVE SELF-TALK FOR FREEDOM FROM WORRY

I never worry. Instead of worrying, I find solutions and I act on them.

My mind is constantly in tune with the positive. It is bright, cheerful, enthusiastic, and full of good, positive thoughts and ideas.

I am able to relax easily and comfortably in my body and in my mind. I am calm, confident, and self-assured.

My mind is orderly and well organized. I consciously choose what I think and I always choose those thoughts that are the most positive and beneficial for me.

All of my thoughts create healthiness within me. My mind dwells only on those thoughts that create more harmony, balance, and well-being within me and in the world around me.

I automatically, and always, think in a decisive and determined way.

I am full of resolution and the absolute assurance of the best possible outcome in everything that I do.

I choose to look at the world around me in the bright, healthy light of optimism and self-assurance.

I do only those things that are best for me. I create the best within myself, I attract the best in others, and I find the best in the world around me.

I willingly, and without fail, take care of the duties and obligations that I have accepted for myself.

I commit only to those responsibilities that I know I can fulfill.
I focus the attention of my mind only on those things that I can do something about. If I cannot affect it or direct it—I accept it.
I keep my mind too busy thinking good, healthy, positive, constructive, and productive thoughts to ever have any time for worry.
I control the thoughts I choose. No thought, at any time, can dwell in my mind without my approval or permission.
I never worry.

For every habit you can come up with that should be changed, there is the right self-talk to change it. But the two examples of habit-changing self-talk we have just seen will give you an idea of how self-talk is constructed and how it covers not only the problem itself, but how it creates the surrounding mental *environment* that feeds and supports the decision to change.

Most of those things we call bad habits are in reality the symptoms of something else that is going on inside of us. They are the result of a broad variety of beliefs we have about ourselves that, when all lumped together, push us into a pattern of behavior that ends up causing problems for us. Self-talk looks at the "whole being" (all of the furniture in our mental apartments) from a holistic point of view. It doesn't just cure the symptom; it changes the problems that *caused* the symptoms in the first place.

TO CHANGE THE HABIT, CHANGE THE WORDS

We *are* creatures of habit. But any habit once learned can be changed. The problem has been that in the past, changing them has been difficult because we were trying to change direction without first changing the old programming. With self-talk we accomplish both: We override the old while we are creating the new.

Choose a habit you would like to change. Don't try to change your life overnight—start off with a minor habit, something small. Then change the words that describe yourself to you. Once you begin, keep at it. It is exciting to watch the changes that take place, to witness the replacement of old habits that once got in the way with the emergence of fruitful, valuable new habits of winning.

CHAPTER EIGHTEEN

Rewiring Attitudes

Everything we do is affected directly or indirectly by our attitudes. A change in a person's attitude can affect just about everything else in that person's life. Even a small shift in "attitude adjustment" can have a profound effect on what we do and how we do it. If you have ever had a son or daughter in school, you know how true that is. A change in attitude can result in a change in grades, dress, habits, and friends.

The better the attitude, the better the results, in almost anything we do. Because attitude affects our feelings and feelings affect what we do and how well we do it, having a good attitude can be the deciding factor in our successes or failures. The right attitude gives us that important edge.

Since our attitudes are the result of our programming, it makes good sense to take a look at the attitudes we are living with, why they are what they are, and which of them we might like to change. Because every attitude we have *directly* affects how we feel about everything around us and what we do about it—our attitudes are *important.* Without the right attitudes we will *never* have the key that unlocks the treasure chest of happiness and success we so badly want and so richly deserve.

Attitudes create the biggest part of the picture we see of ourselves. They are the filters through which we view everything in our sight. Our attitudes are our dispositions—they are the "state of mind" we live in. Our attitudes express themselves through our moods, our temperament, our willingness, and our hesitations.

Our attitudes propel us forward toward our victories or bog us down in defeat. They are the foothold beneath us in every step we take. They are what others see most of the personality within us; they describe us and define us, projecting the image we present to the world around us. Our attitudes make us rich or poor, happy or unhappy, fulfilled or incomplete. They are the single most determining factor in every action we will ever make. We and our attitudes are inextricably combined; *we* are our attitudes and our attitudes are *us*.

HELPING ATTITUDES IN OTHERS

If you are in any way responsible for the development of the attitudes of others—as a manager, parent, teacher, life coach, et cetera—don't expect to change someone else's attitude with "a carrot or a stick" by using incentives, lectures, punishment, complaints, or flattery. Attitudes don't work that way.

For years, business managers have used incentives to boost attitudes to improve productivity or increase sales. But even though they get short-term improvements, the same businesses find that before too long they have to put a new incentive program into effect. They didn't really change any attitudes. They did nothing more than create a short-term, temporary effect in their employees' *outward behavior*—not a change in their attitudes.

If you use an incentive of one kind or another to change an

attitude, it may *appear* to work, but the effect won't last; you will find yourself needing to resupply another incentive each time the previous incentive wears off.

Another time that we frequently use the wrong method to change attitudes is when we are attempting to help someone else improve an attitude that we believe is working against that person. In spite of the fact that school counselors, parents, husbands, wives, managers, and friends frequently tell some individual, "You need to change your attitude," telling someone that has never done any good at all. In fact, just saying that to someone can have the wrong effect. It is negative programming; it will work against the individual instead of for him. It *reconfirms* his pre-programmed belief that all the bad things he already thinks about himself are true. In fact, it is precisely when a person's attitude is "down" that it is the hardest for that person to figure out any way to change it. Why should they? How can they?

Our attitudes are determined by our beliefs—and if we believe we are less than the best, to us that is *fact*. That is reality—that's the way it *is*. Of course, it isn't true at all. It's just true to the person who believes it.

Recall for a moment the natural process by which attitudes are created in each of us: programming creates beliefs, beliefs create attitudes, attitudes create feelings, feelings determine actions, and actions create results. Each of those steps is the logical and expected result of our conditioning. It follows, then, that every attitude we have, good, bad, or indifferent, is the natural result of the programming that preceded it.

Every one of us from time to time suffers from a less than perfect attitude. A "bad attitude" doesn't belong solely to the student who won't study or to the company employee who didn't get a raise, or to the best friend whose personal life has just fallen apart. Attitudes, good and bad, are an everyday part of our lives.

CHANGING ATTITUDES IN YOURSELF

An attitude we might like to change need not be an attitude that is calamitous or extreme—it may be a problem that is quite simple, an attitude that, if fine-tuned just a little, could make some small part of our daily lives work better. And because even the simplest or the most important of our attitudes can be changed by redoing a piece or two of our programming, if we would like to make the change—and we know how to make that programming change—there really isn't any impassable obstacle stopping us from going ahead and doing it.

These attitudes that you have about yourself create one additional important result: The attitudes you have about yourself determine the attitudes you will have about everything else around you. So if you want to change the way you feel about anything else, you have to start first with the attitudes you have about yourself.

As an example we'll use a self-talk script for "personal responsibility." Our attitudes about the part each of us plays in our own earthly destiny are some of the most important attitudes we will ever hold. The difference between having an attitude of accepting responsibility for who we are and what we do, and having an attitude that makes excuses or places our lives in the hands of others, is essential to our ability to achieve a sense of self, and the individual fulfillment that self-responsibility creates within us.

But even considering the importance this one attitude plays in each of our lives, notice how directly, and effectively, even a few self-talk statements can address a subject, simplify it, and begin the reprogramming process of an attitude that is essential to all of us.

SELF-TALK FOR TAKING RESPONSIBILITY FOR YOURSELF

I take full responsibility for everything about me—even the thoughts that I think. I am in control of the vast resources of my own mind.

I alone am responsible for what I do and what I tell myself about me. No one can share this responsibility with me.

I also allow others to accept their responsibilities for themselves and I do not try to accept their responsibilities for them.

I enjoy being responsible. It puts me in charge of being me—and that's a challenge I enjoy.

I allow no one else, at any time, to assume control or responsibility over my life or over anything that I do. My responsibility to others is an extension of my own responsibility to myself.

I choose to leave nothing about me up to chance. When it comes to me—and anything in my life—I choose to CHOOSE.

My choices are mine alone to make for myself. I do not, at any time, allow anyone else to make my choices for me. And I accept full responsibility for every choice and decision I make.

I always meet all of the obligations that I accept. And I accept no obligations that I will not meet.

I am trustworthy. I can be counted on. I have accepted winning responsibility for myself—and I always live up to the responsibilities I accept.

There is no "they" on whom I lay the blame, or with whom I share my own personal responsibilities. I have learned the great secret of mastering my own destiny. I have learned that "they" is "me."

I have no need to make excuses and no one needs to carry my responsibility for me. I gladly carry my own weight—and I carry it well.

Each day I acknowledge and accept the responsibility—not only for my own actions but also for my emotions, my thoughts, and my attitude.

I accept the responsibility for living my life in a way that creates my strength;, my happiness; my positive, healthy beliefs; and for my past, my present, and my future.

That's a good attitude—the kind of attitude that most of us could do with a little more of. It is an attitude that gets us to stand up for ourselves and be counted. It is an attitude that we can, if we choose, effect in our own lives anytime we want. But it is just one attitude of many that each of us can address and put into motion just by reconvincing ourselves—by overriding the old programming that told us that other people, by some stroke of fate, count more than we do.

There are many such attitudes. Some of them are less lofty, and perhaps not as demanding. But they are made up of perhaps the most important self-talk of all—the self-talk of *self-belief.* That is what attitudes are all about.

Here is an example of attitude-changing self-talk that any of us could use from time to time. If I were ever again to teach in a classroom, I would add the lesson of this self-talk to my everyday curriculum. It is one of the most basic and primary forms of self-talk. But the attitude it can create in us touches every part of our lives. It is the fabric from which all success is woven. It is the God-given birthright that all of us were born with, and deserve to retrieve, embrace, enjoy, and possess for the rest of our lives. It restores us and builds us up. It structures our character, sustains our strength, and fortifies our co[illegible]he internal substance of self-belief—it is the self-talk [illegible]m.

SELF-TALK FOR BUILDING S[illegible]M

I really am very special. I like who I am and I feel good about myself.

Although I always work to improve myself and I get better every day, I like who I am today. And tomorrow, when I'm even better, I'll like myself then, *too.*

It's true that there really is no one else like me in the entire world. There never was another me before, and there will never be another me again.

I am unique—from the top of my head to the bottom of my feet. In some ways I may look and act and sound like some others—but I am not them. I am me.

I wanted to be somebody—and now I know I am. I would rather be me than anyone else in the world.

I like how I feel and I like how I think and I like how I do things. I approve of me and I approve of who I am.

I have many beautiful qualities. I have talents and skills and abilities. I have talents that I don't even know about yet. And I am discovering new talents inside myself all the time.

I am positive. I am confident. I radiate good things. If you look closely, you can even see a glow around me.

I am full of life. I like life and I'm glad to be alive. I am a very special person, living at a very special time.

I am intelligent. My mind is *quick and alert and clever and fun. I think good thoughts, and my mind makes things work right for me.*

I have a lot of energy and enthusiasm and vitality. I am exciting and I really enjoy being me.

I like to be around other people and other people like to be around me. People like to hear what I say and know what I think.

I smile a lot. I am happy on the inside and I am happy on the outside.

I am interested in many things. I appreciate all the blessings I have, and the things that I learn, and all the things I will learn today and tomorrow and forever—just as long as I am.

I am warm, sincere, honest, and genuine. I am all of these things and more. And all of these things are me. I like who I am, and I'm glad to be me.

What simple words they are. What truths they tell us about the selves we contain inside of us. Placed within the beliefs of any one individual, those simple words possess a power that few of us have ever hoped to attain. And yet that self-belief, that sense of self-esteem, is available to all of us. Can you imagine living that way each day—and knowing it?

Imagine children growing up with those kinds of words indelibly instilled in their believing, eager young minds. Imagine the world *they* could create. But for today, for now, just imagine beginning to believe the very best about yourself, each day, all of the time, in any circumstance, always being sure of attitudes that support you, give you faith, prop you up, and give you the courage and the conviction to live life in its most fulfilling, most positive way.

If that sounds improbable, let me remind you that it is your *old* programming that tells you it can't work that way. That is because that is what it was wired to believe. And it is wrong.

TAKE STOCK OF YOUR ATTITUDES

Look at your attitudes. Take stock of your beliefs about yourself. Take a mental inventory of your attitudes—good and bad—and decide for yourself which of those attitudes work for you and which do not. The ones you don't want to keep—throw out. Get rid of them. Keep the ones you like. Change the ones you want to change. Take charge of your attitudes. Put yourself back in control. The least that could happen is that you would get a little more of your real self back again.

Start the adventure. Discover the jewels and gems that are part of your own mind. Seek out and find the rich reserve of attitudes within you that have been waiting to step out and live again. Start talking to yourself the *right* way.

Little changes in attitudes can make big changes in life. Your attitudes affect all of the important things around you. They affect how you feel about yourself. They affect your work, your friends, and your loved ones. When your attitudes get better, so does life. If you would like to make a change or two, fixing an attitude and making life a little better isn't a bad place to start.

CHAPTER NINETEEN

Solving Problems and Accomplishing Goals

There is a kind of self-talk that, although it has a positive effect on our habits and our attitudes, is used specifically to fix problems or help us reach our goals. Problems and goals often go hand in hand. "Problems" are usually thought of as those things that get in the way of our goals. For a moment, replace the word "problem" with the word "challenge." Goals create challenges—and challenges create goals.

The self-talk that will help you solve your problems is the same self-talk that will help you reach your goals. To the brain, overcoming problems and accomplishing goals are one and the same. To your subconscious mind, seeing yourself overcoming a challenge, solving a problem, and reaching a goal require the exact same set of directions—the self-talk is the same.

While I do agree that the mind looks at what we call "problems" and what we call "goals" in exactly the same way, I do not agree with those who tell us that all problems are opportunities. Some problems represent potential opportunities, but not all of them. If a man with a gun in his hand were to walk in at this moment and point the gun at your head, that is *not* an opportunity—that is a *problem*.

Just by understanding that the subconscious mind recognizes, accepts, and acts on problems in the exact same way that it helps us reach our goals, we can change, in a positive way, how we look at many of those things in our lives that we have been told are the natural circumstances of life that, when overcome, automatically and naturally result in the achievement of goals. *You cannot solve a problem without reaching an objective.*

THE TRUE MEANING OF "GOALS"

If we want to talk to ourselves in the most productive way, we should also understand the true meaning of the word "goal." It is a word that has often been misused, and it's been given a position of power it doesn't deserve.

There are a number of words in our language that hold an exalted status that the words themselves are not due. As an example, the word "success" too many times has been used to only mean financial wealth. Because we have been told time and time again that that's what success is, many individuals who have been successful in their own way mistook the financial definition as the correct definition. As a result, they saw themselves as failing rather than succeeding.

The word "goal" has become so encumbered with priorities and demands that it makes even the thought of "setting and reaching goals" something of such great importance that we see it as a task that others, possibly more dedicated than ourselves, might undertake, or something we set aside for another day when we have more time to think about it.

Setting goals should be simple. There is nothing wrong with aspiring to reach the highest mountains of "success." But when we set our sights on our great aspirations, we should never fail to recognize the little goals that get us there—the goals that we set almost *unconsciously,* day after day, that help us survive, endure, overcome, maintain, and achieve each day, step by step. They are our wants, our needs, our smallest expectations of ourselves. These are some of the most important goals of all; they are the goals of everyday living.

Our goals should not be limited to setting short-term, medium-term, and long-term objectives. Although the right self-talk can help you reach the loftiest goals you can imagine, for most of us being president or becoming a millionaire is not the kind of goal we deal with on Monday morning.

You may have a goal as practical as losing a little extra weight, doing better at work, getting a promotion, earning more income, saving more of what you earn, getting past depression, getting more organized, writing better business plans, or closing more sales.

YOUR GOALS CAN BE ANYTHING YOU CHOOSE

Goals can be important and life-altering, or as simple as having more free time, attending church more regularly, running a better household, getting good grades, having better personal relationships, being healthier, going to the symphony, writing a letter home, sending flowers a little more often, doing something special for someone else, looking good for the class reunion, smiling more often, conquering your slice in golf, or catching more fish.

Your goals, and the problems standing between you and those goals, can be anything at all, large or small. But your subconscious mind deals with all of them in the same matter-of-fact and accepting way. If you want to achieve them, give yourself the right directions, the right words—take advantage of your own mind's natural dedication to do for you what you tell it most.

To solve any problem or reach any goal, great or small, the internal [illegible] process we go through is the same. If you want to be bet[illegible] job, lose weight, or create wealth in your life, it is all the [illegible] your subconscious mind. To it, one direction is the same [illegible]ther. The more programming it receives to help you reac[illegible]jective you present it with, the more it will move in that [illegible]

To illustrat[illegible] we target a specific problem or goal, let's look at an exa[illegible]ome self-talk that addresses the broader area of how [illegible]roblems in general—what we believe about the pro[illegible]counter in any given day. How we look at our [illegible] an important role in what we do about them. [illegible]void, confront, go around them—or solve the[illegible]

It does[illegible]erence to our internal computer what the [illegible]blem is or how big it is. But what we tell ourselves about our problems will affect every action we take from that moment forward.

SOLVING PROBLEMS

The following are a few words of self-talk for how to deal with the problem of solving problems.

I'm good at solving problems. I like challenges and I meet them head-on.

Problems are my teachers. They help me to learn and grow. Without them, I would be going nowhere. With them, I am moving forward in the direction of my own goals.

There is no problem that I cannot conquer. I am strong in mind, body, and spirit. My will, my strength, and my determination are always greater than any problem I face.

When I meet a new problem, I do not see the problem as my enemy. I know that finding the solution to the problem will move me forward in my own personal growth.

Because I know that problems are key ingredients in my spiritual and mental education and preparation, I recognize that all problems are important to me.

I do not fear problems, I solve them. I do not ignore problems, I confront them. I do not avoid problems, I conquer them.

I know that every problem holds within itself the key to its own solution. Therefore, the better I understand the problem, the clearer I am able to see its solution.

Having problems is not a problem for me. I am confident, self-assured, positive, and determined. I always know that I am going to overcome any problem I encounter—and I always do.

I am good at breaking large obstacles down into smaller pieces that are easier to handle. And I never make any problem appear to be larger than it actually is.

I never worry. I turn "worry time" into positive, constructive "solution time." I keep my mind alert and open to all solutions—and solutions come quickly and easily to me.

I have learned to recognize that many problems carry with them benefits and potential opportunities that would not have presented themselves had the problem not occurred in the first place.

I do not seek to live a life that is free from all problems. Instead, I choose to live a life of finding solutions and enjoying the benefits that those solutions create.

"Challenge," "conquer," "solution," and "win" are words that I live by daily. "Challenges" are opportunities. "Conquering" them is the inevitable outcome.

> *"Solutions" are the stepping-stones to my success. "Winning" is my way of life.*

I suspect you will find that if you were to do nothing more than read that one example of a self-talk script to yourself three or four times each day [illegible] eek or two, by the end of that time you would begin t [illegible] r own problems differently—even though the exampl [illegible] alk we have just used do not tackle a specific problem. [illegible] ly with your general approach to looking at problem [illegible]

Now let's be m [illegible]. Let's identify a problem—one that for many of [illegible] time or another, stood directly in the way of reac [illegible] t any goal we set for ourselves: the problem of being [illegible]—managing our time and our resources in a more [illegible] nd productive way.

There are ma [illegible] ent books on the subject of managing time and bec [illegible] more organized. But when you read the books, think [illegible] much better a more receptive mind would be—a mi [illegible] hat has become reprogrammed, firmly convinced, regardless of what you might have believed in the past, to now believe that being organized is a natural way for you to be.

If your goal was to organize your thoughts, your time, and your activities to get more done for you, and help you reach the rest of the goals you have set for yourself instead of following the old programming, it is just as easy and far more effective to use a different set of internal commands.

> *I am organized and in control of my life. I am in control of myself, my thoughts, my time, my actions, and my future.*
>
> *I know what to do and when to do it, and I do everything I need to do, when I need to do it.*

I program my mind to make the maximum use of my time. I am in control of my time and how to use it. I like being organized, efficient, and on top of things.

Controlling my time keeps me that way.

I never waste time—I always "plan" time. And because I plan my time, I always have time to do the things I choose to do.

Each day I become more organized and in control of all areas of my life—at home, at work, in my mind and in my thoughts, in everything that I do.

I am very well organized. Each night I make a list of things I need to do the next day. I set my priorities and I follow them.

I am always on time. I am always right where I need to be, exactly when I need to be there.

Being on time is easy for me and the more I control my time and the more organized I become, the easier it is.

I am in control of my feelings, my emotions, my attitudes, and my needs. I control them; they do not control me.

I have the winning vote in the outcome of my own actions. And I choose to live my life by choice, not chance. Therefore, I take the time to take control.

I have an organized and orderly mind. Because I think in an organized way, I conduct my life in an organized manner.

I think in the most positive and productive way at all times and in all things. The way I think is the way I live—and I think "right."

I am the director of my destiny. I know where I am going and I know why I am going there. My earthly life is in my hands and in my control.

I control my goals and the achievement of my goals. I organize my goals by writing each of them down, along with the steps I need to reach them. One of the reasons for my success is that my goals are clearly defined and organized.

I am in complete control of what I think and how I think. Therefore, I choose to think only those thoughts that help me and that are of genuine benefit to me.

Even after years of working with self-talk—writing, recording, and helping people put self-talk into practice—I still focus on the importance of its directness; the more simple and to the point your self-talk is, the better it works.

As an example, when I was working on the recorded sessions of *Self-Talk for Weight-Loss,* the importance of using explicit, direct wording proved to be essential. While writing the actual self-talk for the goal of losing weight and keeping it off, I identified a list of subject areas of self-talk—each of which was vital to the one specific goal I was writing about. The list of weight-loss subjects included such areas as *"Getting Started," "Sitting Down to Eat," "Learning to Say No," "Health and Fitness," "Self-Talk for Exercising," "Self-Esteem for Weight Loss,"* and *"Taking Control of Your Life."*

Each of the subject areas covered required a self-talk script that dealt directly with that one area of the problem. Each of the scripts was written to deal with every part and facet of that area. The individual scripts had to cover all of the details that contribute to creating the overall problem.

As an example of how explicit and direct the right kind of self-talk should be, I'll give you a few of the actual self-talk self-directions from one of the scripts I wrote for weight loss. This particular segment deals with a problem—and a goal—that everyone who has ever had a problem with weight has had to deal with at one time or another, the problem of "Sitting Down to Eat." It begins with the important self-direction of being in control, and then dives into the *details* of the problem.

I am in control of myself in every way—at all times and in all situations.

Each time I sit down to eat I reaffirm my determination to achieve my goal. By eating right, and never giving in, I am reaching the weight I want.

Whether eating in or eating out, I really enjoy eating less.

I never feel the need to finish the food in front of me. I eat only what I should—and never one bite more.

One way to weight loss that's easy and works is less food on my plate and less on my fork.

By ordering less when I eat out, and by serving myself smaller portions at home, I keep myself aware of the importance of staying with my goal—each and every day. Less on my plate means less on my waist.

When I sit down to eat, at no time do I allow anyone else to influence, tempt, or discourage me in any negative way.

What I eat, and the goals I reach, are up to me. And I give no one the right to hinder or control my success.

Although others may benefit from my success, I am achieving my weight-loss goals for my own personal reasons—for myself, my life, my future, and my own personal well-being.

I am never, at any time, tempted to take one bite more than I should. I am strong, I am capable of reaching my goal, and I am doing it.

Being in situations that put a lot of food in front of me is not a problem to me now. I simply say "No" to the food and "Yes" to my success.

I enjoy sitting down to eat. Each time I do, I conquer my past, and I create a trimmer, happier, more self-confident future in front of me.

When I sit down to eat, I do not need someone else to remind me of my goal, or to keep me from eating something I should not. I take full responsibility for myself, and no one else has to do it for me.

Controlling my weight, and my appetite, is easy for me now. I enjoy smaller portions, smaller bites, and a slower, healthier, more relaxed way of eating.

I have set my goal and I am staying with it. I have turned mealtime into "achievement time."

That's the kind of healthy new self-talk that, when practiced even for a short period of time, begins to automatically step in to replace the earlier programs that kept us from reaching the goal we wanted to reach. Once you become conditioned to making that simple shift in what you say to yourself, the new self-directions come, almost without thinking about them.

BE SPECIFIC—FIX THE PROBLEM

The key to good self-talk is that it covers the problem—and it gets specific. When you want to fix a problem, *fix the problem.* When you want to achieve precise goals, even the little ones, givc your brain clear commands.

Those of us whose dream it is to improve our lives, even in some small way, can do so. If you want to solve a problem (meet a challenge) or reach any goal, learn to give yourself precise and complete directions. If you have a goal, no matter what it is, wire your brain with detailed instructions that tell you exactly what you want. And then stand back and get out of the way. Your expectations are about to happen.

CHAPTER TWENTY

Self-Motivation

People who are the most successful at whatever they do are those who are their own best motivators. They stand on their own feet, get themselves moving, and put themselves in charge of their own success.

Instead of relying on the outside world to motivate you, think how much better it would be if you could always rely on yourself for that same motivation. If you wire in the right words to use when you talk to yourself, you can easily learn to give yourself the motivation you need, anytime you need it.

Here are a few examples. This first script of self-talk for motivation is the kind of self-talk that is designed to get you emotionally "up." It talks to you *about you* in a way that gets you moving, while it supports that motivation with self-talk that gives you extra belief in yourself. You are not only programming yourself to meet the challenge, you are also giving yourself the extra insurance of the added belief that you can and will accomplish the task you are setting out to do.

This is self-talk that anyone can use at any time. It is not specific to any one area of motivation—making more sales, getting up on time, scoring points in a basketball game, or getting caught … paperwork—but it will work for all of these and mo… self-talk that will give your subconscious mind a n… rections that will help you motivate yourself in any are… fe.

I can do … believe I can do. I've got it and every day I get more … ve talent, skills, and ability.

I set goals … h them. I know what I want out of life. I go after it and …

People like m… eel good about myself. I have a sense of pride in who … d I believe in myself.

Nothing seems t… ne. I have a lot of determination. I turn problems into advantages. I find possibilities in things that other people never give a chance.

I have a lot of energy—I am very alive. I enjoy life and I can tell it and so can others. I keep myself up, looking ahead, and liking it.

I know that I can accomplish anything I choose, and I refuse to let anything negative hold me back or stand in my way.

I am not afraid of anything or anyone. I have strength, power, conviction, and confidence. I like challenges and I meet them head-on, face-to-face—today especially.

I am on top of the world and I'm going for it. I have a clear picture in my mind of what I want. I can see it in front of me. I know what I want and I know how to get it. I know that it's all up to me and I know I can do it.

Roadblocks don't bother me. They just mean that I am alive and running, and I'm not going to stand still for anything.

I trust myself. I've got what it takes—plenty of it—and I know how to use it. Today more than ever. Today I am unstoppable. I've got myself together and I'm getting more together every day. And today—look out world, here I come.

Limitations? I don't even recognize them as limitations. There is *no challenge I can't conquer. There* is *no wall I can't climb over. There* is *no problem I can't defeat or turn around and make it work for me.*

I stand tall. I am honest and sincere. I like to deal with people and they like me. I think well; I think clearly. I am organized; I am in control of myself, and everything about me.

I call my shots and no one has to call them for me. I never blame anyone else for the circumstances of my life. I accept my failings and move past them as easily as I accept the rewards for my victories.

I never demand perfection of myself, but I expect the very best of what I have to give—and that's what I get.

I never give myself excuses. I get things done on time and in the right way. Today I have the inner strength to do more than ever.

I am an exceptional human being. My goals and my incredible belief in myself turn my goals into reality. I have the power to live my dreams. I believe in them like I believe in myself. And that belief is so strong that there is nothing that diminishes my undefeatable spirit.

Try reading *that* to yourself out loud each morning. Wouldn't it be wonderful if we had someone who believed in us so much that every day we could count on being told those incredible, motivating truths about ourselves? If we had that, we would certainly have the truest and best friend we could ever find.

The truth is, of course, we *do* have that friend. Each of us does. Right here inside ourselves. All we have to do is ask and our friend will be there, without fail, at any time, in any circumstance.

GIVING LIFE TO YOUR SELF-TALK

When you first read these new words of self-belief and self-motivation, they can lie there on the page, looking like not much more than quietly reassuring inspirational thoughts. Bring them to life. Pull them off the page. Shout them out to yourself if you have to, but grab them, hold on to them, and make them your own.

If you're going to shock your subconscious with the new words, you might as well give it a full dose. Instead of ever letting the de-motivators in your life weaken you or bring you to your knees, even for a moment, kick them out. Stand up, face them, point to the door, and tell them to get out of your life. You're through with them, and you don't need them any longer. Stop them in *their* tracks. Overpower them.

Just when your subconscious thinks you're through, don't let up, give it some more. And this time start by making the conscious decision to *demand* that the internal you *listens very carefully.*

I know that greatness begins in the minds of the great. I know that what I believe about myself is what I will become—so I believe in the best for myself.

I am practical and realistic, and I keep my feet on solid ground. But I also give myself the freedom to live up to my fullest expectations.

I never limit myself by the shortsighted beliefs of others—instead I open myself up to the broad horizons of unlimited possibility.

When someone says I "cannot," I answer, "Why not?" When someone says, "It's impossible," I answer that nothing is any more impossible than I believe it to be. And I truly believe that with my individual fortress of faith in me, anything is possible.

I have drive, spirit, stamina, and endurance. I have a good, strong winning attitude about myself and about everything I do. I am practical and realistic, but I also believe in the best possible outcome of any situation.

If I have ever had any doubts about myself in the past, today is a good day to put them aside. It's a good day to throw out any disbelief that ever held me back.

I know that I am headed in the right winning direction, and I look forward and never look back. I have the ability to focus on one thing at a time, so I concentrate my attention on the job at hand—and I get it done.

Today is one of those days when nothing *can stand in my way. When I need extra determination, I've got it. When I need more energy and drive, I've got it. I've got the power to get it done and the patience to see it through, no matter what the job or challenge may be.*

Right now, even while I am telling myself these truths about me, I know that I can succeed and I am succeeding. At this moment, if I think of any challenge in front of me, I know that I will become even more of a winner because of it.

I keep my chin up, my head held high. I look, act, sound, think, and feel like the winner I am. Anytime a problem starts to get me down, I get myself right back up. I tackle problems and I solve them. When frustration or defeat threatens me, I just become that much stronger, more positive, better organized, and more determined than ever.

Right now, today, this very moment, I am capable of giving myself the gift of absolute self-assurance, self-belief, and powerful nonstop confidence in myself.

No matter what it is that requires the very best of me, I can do it and I know I can.
Today is a great day. And I've got what it takes. So I choose to do it right, do it well. I choose to live today with joy and love.
I know it's all up to me. One hundred percent. Every bit of it. All of it is in how I look at it and what I do about it. That's what winning is. That's why I am a winner.
I set my sights. I keep my balance. I don't hesitate. I don't hold back. I know that the world is full of opportunities. Look at what I can do, look at where I can go. Look at what I can do just by saying "Yes" to myself.
Just look at what I can do today. I am incredible . . . and today is a great day to show it.

It is easy to see how that kind of self-direction can be worded to apply specifically to any part of your life that needs to be motivated.

SELF-TALK FOR SELLING

One of the professions that relies heavily on motivation is the sales field. We know that salespeople need to maintain a constant attitude of self-belief because of the number of times they are turned down; every time the competition wins, or when the prospect says no, the salesperson loses. In the mind of the salesperson who lost the sale, that loss represents a failure. Because of this, the field of sales creates the largest demand for skilled, professional motivators.

If you are in a management or sales position, read this next example of self-talk carefully. But even if you are not in the field of professional sales, notice how much of the self-talk for selling applies equally as well to the ti vhen you want to influence or persuade sc ay of thinking or to do something that *you*

For this example, I wil reas of sales self-talk and show you just a presentative of the self-talk for selling.

I begin each day with a clear mind and a specific plan to get the most from my time and my effort. I follow my plan and I reach my goals.

An accurate description of me would include the words "professional, hardworking, qualified, skillful, energetic, enthusiastic, organized, determined, and highly successful."

I am good at persuading others to my point of view. That is because I first and always recognize and understand the point of view of the individual to whom I am presenting my ideas, my product, or my service.

I know how to listen—and I do. I have learned to not only hear the words that are being said, but also listen to the unspoken thoughts that lie behind them.

I am always prepared. I take the time to do it right. In everything I do, I am prepared, confident, self-assured, and successful.

I always take care of the details in my work. I enjoy the details of selling and I always tend to them on time and with full attention.

I keep myself "up." I know that making good sales presentations means keeping myself up, energetic, and in control. That is exactly the way I am, and my sales presentations are always professional and effective.

I never avoid confronting a problem or making a sales call of any kind. I keep myself working and that keeps me winning.

I deserve to make the sales I create. I know that success in selling starts with seeing myself as the capable, productive individual that I am.

I am always sincere and honest. I believe that all achievement in selling begins with trust, skill, and determination. I ask for the order frequently and without hesitation. At every "buying signal," I ask for the order—and I close.

Being told "no" never bothers me. Instead, hearing the word "no" doubles my determination and adds to my positive enthusiasm.

Given the technical skills to match, the salesperson who mentally "becomes" the individual we have just described, even in those few short self-directives, would undoubtedly rank high on the list of sales achievers for any sales organization. Having worked with many salespeople in the past, I have all too often heard quite the opposite kinds of self-talk.

Because of our own past programming, it is all too easy to slip into using the old self-talk de-motivators of complaints, excuses, and doubts—all the reasons necessary to place the blame for failure and underachievement on someone or something else: the sales manager, the company, the leads, the commission structure, or the competition.

Instead of igniting the spark of self-belief, too many salespeople, just like many of us in our own careers, solve the day's problems by avoiding the action we know we should take. Instead of spending a few minutes engaged in the highly productive activity of motivating ourselves to take action, we engage ourselves in talking ourselves *out* of action, and into having another cup of coffee.

TIME TO BEGIN

We can learn to motivate ourselves. We can learn to become self-starters, doers, and achievers. To do that takes less time and less training than any other kind of motivational development I have ever encountered. We need only to begin, and our inner selves, the part of us that *wants* to achieve, will soon begin to follow the new lead that we are giving it.

CHAPTER TWENTY-ONE

Situational Self-Talk

When I first explored the use of "situational" self-talk, I couldn't help but wonder if it was possible that something so simple could work so well. I was aware from studying and observing many different self-help techniques, however, that the most effective techniques were usually the *simplest* and the easiest to use. That description fits situational self-talk perfectly. If this form of self-talk seems too uncomplicated to be valuable, I urge you to try it for yourself for the next three weeks. By the end of that time, you should already be forming the habit of doing it—and it will no longer seem unimportant. It will become one of your strongest allies in your own personal growth and success. What is this simple key that unlocks such a great treasure?

MAKE AN INSTANT ADJUSTMENT

A friend of mine related the story of her aunt, who, although she did not like to cook, had to do so to take care of her family. Each time the aunt went into the kitchen to begin preparing a meal, she would say out loud, "This is going to be fun. I'm going to have a good time cooking today." When it comes to wiring your brain, think about the effect of repeating that kind of statement. By giving herself a few simple words of self-talk, that woman changed a chore into a pleasant task. She didn't change the job; she changed how she felt about it.

That is situational self-talk. *It is the kind of self-talk that adjusts situations by adjusting how we look at them.* It is a practical, immediate, *now* kind of self-talk that you can call on at any time and it will come to your aid the moment you use it.

Situational self-talk differs from the kinds of self-talk we discussed in the last few chapters in that it does not require a "script" of self-talk to create a result. It can be accomplished in a moment, out loud or silently to yourself. It can be a single thought, or it can be a few well-chosen words.

Situational self-talk also differs from the other forms of positive self-talk in that it doesn't have to be phrased in the present tense only. It is already dealing with the here and now, today, or the near future. Its first objective is not to try to create a new, long-term internal picture of yourself; its primary job is to deal with today, *today.* So when you say to yourself, "I'm going to enjoy going to work today," the words you are using are *future* tense (going to), but they are still dealing with *now*.

Like the other kinds of self-talk, this "in the moment" form may help your attitude, overpower a bad habit, help you solve a problem or reach a goal, or motivate you to do better, but it accomplishes the task in a different way.

Situational self-talk is used when you are confronted with any situation that you would rather not be in, or when you are presented with an unexpected opportunity that requires your immediate attention. In most cases this kind of self-talk is used to overcome some momentary circumstance that disagrees with you. I'll give you an example.

You are at work, and the phone rings. It is a call from someone you've been putting off talking to, and you know you need to take the call. You don't want to, but you know the problem has to be met with sooner or later. You have the choice of talking to the person or putting the confrontation off until another time. By then, the problem probably will have gotten worse. What you do next is your choice; the decision to take the call or put it off is entirely up to you.

It is at a time like this when just a few words of the right kind of self-talk can help you do the right thing. Instead of saying to yourself, "Oh, no, not him again. Tell him I'll call him back," you can use self-talk to tackle the problem then and there.

> *I like solving problems. I always deal with problems and I never avoid them. I'll take the call and I'll tackle the problem head-on.*

I am often convinced that situational self-talk, this seemingly simplest form of self-talk, is at times the most valuable of all. If you are consciously practicing the other forms of self-talk for getting your life together and working at improving yourself in other important ways, using situational self-talk becomes an almost automatic by-product of the other self-talk you are using. But unless you are aware of this special kind of self-talk, you may not recognize how easy it is to use and how much good it can do for you.

DRIVING YOURSELF TO DISTRACTION

Years ago, I fit into the category of individuals who give themselves minor emotional fits when they are driving in traffic. I know people who verbalize near-obscenities (or worse) at traffic lights that change at the wrong time or at other drivers who do the wrong things, like pulling in front of them or cutting them off. When they are going somewhere and are about to be late they hit, with equal force, the brake, the gas pedal, and the horn.

It doesn't seem to have a lot to do with how important it is that they didn't get started on time. Behind the steering wheel all vengeance is meted out with equal fury. After this emotional driving style becomes a habit, these otherwise fine individuals get so used to driving with stress that they clutch the steering wheel with the same Indianapolis 500 grip even when they aren't late for anything or when they are going nowhere in particular.

A friend of mine, the owner of a successful business in the Los Angeles area, is, in his normal waking state, one of the coolest, most staid individuals I have ever met. He is always kind, considerate, deferent, and understanding—except when he is trying to change lanes on a Los Angeles freeway and someone unwittingly pulls in front of him.

My basic belief in the goodness of humanity tells me that the young man driving the secondhand car who pulls into the wrong position in front of my friend's late-model foreign import on the freeway is probably an okay person. If he only knew what expletives had just been expressed on his behalf! And then, moments later, my friend is once again his cool, calm, caring, and collected self. That is, until the next unfortunate soul steers his car in the wrong direction, and my friend once again unleashes a torrent of temper on the unsuspecting driver of the other vehicle.

Before I had self-talk completely figured out and made it a way of life in my own life, my own particular automotive stress-builders were stoplights and slow-moving traffic. One day, while driving to my office and being a little late, I found myself anxiously anticipating the change in *every* traffic light I encountered between my home and my office. Halfway there, I came to the astonishing realization that I was doing my attitude, and probably my health, a great injustice. More than that, I realized that my behavior was not that which should be expected of a mature adult; I was dealing with traffic at about the same level that an eighteen-month-old child deals with hunger. I was actually *creating* the stress and unconsciously affecting my attitude in a negative way.

As soon as this realization hit me I made an instant decision. I decided that never again would traffic, in any situation, cause me stress. I immediately reinforced my decision with a few simple lines of situational self-talk.

I enjoy relaxing while I am driving the car.

I always give myself the necessary amount of time to get anywhere I am going. I always arrive at—or before—the time I need to be there.

Traffic lights change at their own discretion: not mine. If the light changes before I get there, I will stop, wait for the light to change, and relax while I am waiting.

Slow-moving or standing traffic is not a problem to me. I enjoy the time I have to organize my thoughts and think about those things that are beneficial to me. I will get there when I get there.

By practicing this each time the opportunity came up, the self-talk took hold. In time I wired negative driving self-talk out of my brain and replaced it with a new attitude that still drives with me today. It was so obvious and simple to do, I might have completely overlooked it.

THE CHEMICALS OF STRESS

What aggravation we give ourselves! What emotions we force ourselves to endure. Mind/brain researchers have gained great insight into the process of the effect of the *natural* chemicals our brains trigger and dump into our systems—just from a few minutes of negative emotional stress. (I have pointed out to my seminar audiences that, as an example of the effects of negative stress, a ten-minute argument in the morning with someone close to us dumps enough toxic levels of chemicals into our system that it takes eight *hours* for our system just to get back to normal.)

If a few *minutes* of anger, anxiety, negative stress, or frustration can literally add chemical toxins that last for hours to our physical systems, why do we do it? Why do we let ourselves get out of control? We do it because we thought it was okay to be that way; we grew up not quite shaking off the last vestiges of immaturity.

We kept a few of the negative behavior styles of our childhood with us so we could trot them back out when things don't go the way we'd like them to go. In businesses, I have seen some usually levelheaded people, from the CEO to the first-time assistant, momentarily throw their sanity out the window because life, at that moment, wasn't the way they wanted it to be.

We are all human. But there is nothing stopping us from stepping past a human frailty or two and rising above the crowd. If people around you choose to let situations and circumstances control them, there probably is not too much you can do about it. But you *can* do something about yourself—how you deal with every situation you confront, every unexpected jack-in-the-box complication, and every circumstance in your life that you cannot change or control.

All of us have dozens of things we would like to change—in our jobs, in our personal lives, at home, at school, with our friends, with the rules and laws we live by, with those who govern us, with how we spend our time—with everything about us.

CONSCIOUS ACTIONS OR UNCONTROLLED REACTIONS

How we react to those things in life that we can do nothing about will always be a test of our own self-control. I am frequently amazed at the number of people who consistently complain about things they can do nothing about. How often we hear someone complain about something as totally uncontrollable as the *weather*! We have all known someone who let rain or an overcast sky ruin an entire day. The weather does exactly what it wants to do; the loudest complaint won't change it. Complaining about anything out of our control is not only senseless, but the negative self-talk we use to lodge the complaint has a direct effect on how we function that day—mentally *and* physically.

It is so much easier and healthier to recognize the reality of the situation as it actually is (such as weather), and adjust our own self-talk to accept it and possibly even enjoy it. Why not? It's going to rain anyway. Try looking at it differently. Give yourself a few words of self-talk that will direct your subconscious and conscious minds to see things differently, at least for that day.

It's raining today, and that's fine with me. I'm going to have a good day, and a little rain can't stop me.

There is an increasing amount of scientific evidence that tells us that something as simple as having a good attitude is much more than just a good idea.

We've known for years that having a good frame of mind makes things work better for us. But we now know that something as incidental as having the right frame of mind plays a part in a mental and biological chain reaction that involves every facet of *what* we are and *who* we are—every moment, throughout our entire lives.

Research in the field of neuroscience has proved that such things as thoughts, moods, attitudes, and actions play a far more important role in our mental and physical chemistry than we had ever thought possible. For us, the beneficiaries of this field of scientific research, the conclusions can be startling. How important are a few casual thoughts? They are more important than we had ever imagined.

Our biological environment, our physical makeup and health, affects our state of mind. The better condition our internal biological environment is in, the better we think and act. And the more productively we think, the more positively we affect ourselves emotionally and physically.

THE SITUATION CYCLE

Just the simple act of telling yourself you are going to have a "good day," as an example, not only helps convince you mentally, it sets off chemical/electrical triggers in your brain that affect your mental state, which in turn affects you physiologically, which in turn affects how you think.

It is a self-generating cycle: thought, emotional response, physiological response, thought, emotional response, and so on, until something breaks or changes the cycle. That is why one negative incident, first thing in the morning, can cause a chain reaction that, if left unchecked, can affect everything else throughout the day. It affects our energy and our enthusiasm, our initiative and our spirit.

The implication of this is that you can successfully scuttle an entire day by allowing even a single event to create the first step in a negative cycle. This negative cycle is not caused by the problem or event that appears to set it off—the cycle begins with how you *respond* to the problem in the first place.

That is why it's just not practical, physiologically or mentally, to complain or get "down" about normal daily irritations—or any of the things you can do nothing about. But you *can,* instead, within moments, change how you feel about them. Instead of creating a *negative* cycle, you can create a *positive* cycle anytime you choose. For most of us, creating positive cycles is a far more enjoyable way to make it through the day.

Of course, we've all met those individuals who seem to enjoy being miserable. No matter how well things are going for them, they will find something to help them feel unhappy. Fortunately, most of us like to feel good. We would rather be happy than unhappy—we would rather feel good than feel bad. And the truth is, anyone can feel happy or unhappy, in tune or out of control, almost anytime they want to. Your own internal self-talk is not a magic solution for every situation that comes up, but it can help you stay in control and deal with each of them more realistically and more effectively.

We should not expect ourselves to have smiles on our faces every moment of the day. But I suspect that all of us would fare better at life by working at smiling a little more—maybe a lot more.

MAKING THE *BEST* OF LESS-THAN-THE-BEST

There are times, however, when we are faced with situations that are quite normal but do not call for a countenance of eternal bliss. If you have ever taken a child into the emergency room at eleven o'clock at night and left an hour later with your child sixteen stitches stronger and your bank account several hundred dollars poorer, you know what I mean.

If that happened to you, imagine what would be going on in your mind. Even if the injury was not serious, you would be concerned. When the child came running in with the injury, whatever you were doing would have been immediately interrupted and you would probably spend the next hour or two sitting in the waiting area at the emergency room. It would not be the perfect ending to a beautiful day.

If that situation happened to you, how would you feel? What unconscious thoughts would you say to yourself? More than likely your emotions would be running somewhere between anger, concern, and being just plain upset!

What you say to yourself at a time like that will affect the frame of mind you are in, how you feel, and how well you handle the situation—and yourself. How well your son or daughter does will depend on the doctor and whatever words of encouragement you can offer. How well *you* do is entirely up to you! If you have made the decision to be in control of yourself, you will talk to yourself in the right way—immediately, directly, realistically, and positively.

Situational self-talk doesn't expect you to instantly change every bad situation into a good situation. It simply gives you a way to consciously put the best construction on any situation. It keeps you in control—of yourself—and allows you to function at your best under any circumstance that comes along.

Have you ever been driving alone when you had a flat tire? I would wager that the self-talk that happens next is usually less than the best kind.

If you have a spare, and can change the tire yourself, you pull over, get out, open the trunk, wrestle the spare to the ground, find the jack and fight it out of its hiding place, jack up the car, force the hubcap from its locked-in position, physically and verbally fight the nuts off the wheel lugs, jockey the spare onto the hub, replace the nuts, pound the hubcap back into place, get back into the car, and continue on your way.

The self-talk that goes on from the moment we have the flat tire to some time after, perhaps long after, either keeps us in control and keeps our spirits up, or, as happens in most circumstances like this, our own words, our own thoughts, make the problem worse.

All too often, the words we have said to ourselves when things went wrong *contributed* to the problem—instead of making it better or helping us solve it. If you think about it, have you ever seen anyone whistling, humming a happy tune, or smiling while changing a flat tire on the side of the road?

ENDLESS OPPORTUNITIES TO BREAK *OR MAKE* YOUR DAY

Things that get us upset can be anything and everything. Each day we are confronted with an obstacle course of endless possibilities of things that could upset us, make us angry, or drive us to distraction—if we let them. The daily events that occur in the lives of even a few of us would give us an almost endless list of daily frustrations. The results of just one or two of them happening to us can create, with the wrong kind of self-talk, reason enough to get thrown off course. If the frustration is big enough, it can ruin the whole day.

Situational self-talk may not change the problem, but if used consciously and immediately the moment the need arises, it can rapidly change how we respond to the problem at hand and how we navigate the rest of the day. Some of these situations are important, but some of them can be so petty that it's hard to see how they could upset us at all. What they all have in common is the way we react to them.

They are the causes of arguments, frustrations, anxiety, stress, and bad days—and they can be anything at all, large or small: the toast is burned; the plane is late; the boss is giving you a hard time; one of the kids came home with a bad report card; you're halfway through your shower and you run out of hot water; your favorite television program got preempted; you're late for work and you can't find anything to wear; your promotion didn't come through, et cetera. Are the things that go wrong all that bad? To our subconscious minds they are exactly as bad—or as good—as we perceive them to be, as we tell ourselves they are.

Instead of getting needlessly upset and thereby starting a negative cycle, when you have to wait in line, practice saying something different to yourself. Instead of thinking, *I hate standing in line,* it is just as easy to use some self-talk to change how you look at standing in lines. If you wonder if it works, try it the next chance you get.

I don't mind standing in line. That's where I am and I'm doing what I need to do. Standing in line doesn't bother me—and I really like getting things done.

I know people who hate to get a voicemail message when they are trying to reach someone on the telephone. "I hate voicemail" is the program they have convinced themselves to believe. Actually, voicemail isn't all that bad. It helps a lot of people stay in touch when they can't answer their phones. It serves its purpose. We can decide to let reaching voicemail instead of a live person upset us or we can recognize that it is a part of our technology and decide to accept it and make it okay.

Telling yourself that you don't like to talk to an electronic message won't stop people from using voicemail. It can't, for the present, be changed. What you can change is how you respond to it: "I'm glad I have the chance to leave a message."

IT IS AS IT IS

Whatever the example, it doesn't matter whether we are in the camp of those who like the way the situation is or not. If it is a situation that *is,* then it *is*!

I know people who do not like to wear seat belts when they are driving or riding in a car. They can be heard to proclaim every possible reason why they should not have to wear them. The reasons range from how seat belts wrinkle their clothes or how uncomfortable they are to saying that wearing them should be an individual choice, not a law. But if you want to follow the rules, you have the choice of telling yourself what a nuisance you think they are or telling yourself that they don't bother you at all. They can be a daily grievance or they can be nothing more than a safety device that is there—and there is no need to give it a negative second thought.

Just as situational self-talk will work for the smallest of inconveniences, it will work equally well in more important circumstances—those, as an example, that directly affect our income and our professional growth. When I work with corporations and businesses, I hear grievances and resentments from individuals at every level of the corporate structure. Most of them are expressions of dissatisfaction with things that the individual can do nothing about. It may be company policy, government regulation, or a manager's actions—all of which are a part of normal business life.

The positive self-talker soon learns to recognize the unchangeable realities of business. He not only makes the best of them and stops fighting them—consciously and unconsciously—but gets busy helping the company move ahead so he can have a good place to work and an opportunity to further his career. After spending many years in business environments, I could fill several chapters of a book discussing techniques and methods to overcome the obstacles of personal attitudes and the application of self-talk to enhance productivity in our jobs and careers. Just imagine what making minor, daily attitude shifts could do for us on the job!

I have never tried to estimate the number of major and minor problems and upsets the average individual faces in a month or a year. There is no need to dwell on them; we all have enough examples of our own. I've used just a few examples to give you the idea. I am sure by now you have thought of your own examples. Think of anything in your day that gets in the way, and you'll find an opportunity that could use some situational self-talk.

There are even times when others around us will use any persuasive techniques possible to get us thinking in the right direction. I remember the story of the brilliant woman who dented the fender of her husband's new sports car. The car was his pride and joy, and the smallest nick in the paint would be a calamity to him. When she arrived home, she rushed into the house in hysterics saying, "I've just had the most horrible accident and I've wrecked your car!" The husband, who was instantly concerned for his wife's safety, was greatly relieved when she assured him, through her tears, that she had come out of the wreck unscathed.

Caught between his concern for his wife's well-being and agonizing over the loss of the car, the husband finally asked her where the car was now.

"It's in the driveway," she said, still trying to calm herself down. The husband, worried and shaken, put his arm around his wife and together they walked out to the driveway to view the battered remains of his shiny new car. When he saw the small dent in the fender, his worst fears turned to joyous elation. "It's nothing at all! I'm just glad you weren't hurt. We can get it fixed—look, it's just a small dent! It's hardly even noticeable!"

If the wife had, instead, walked into the house and announced, "I just put a dent in your new car," I am sure the husband's reaction would have been a little different. I suspect that his self-talk that evening would not have been thoughts of relief and thankfulness. In this instance, the wife, who had obviously figured out her husband pretty well, set up his self-talk for him. Most of the time, however, we are not so well set up: We have to find our own self-talk and fend for ourselves.

If the husband had been a practiced, positive self-talker in the first place, his wife could have used a more direct approach to the problem. The important point is that our responses to situations are based on what we perceive—what we say to ourselves either consciously or unconsciously at the time. The dent in the fender, it turned out, was not the issue. The position the husband took, *internally,* was.

THE NEXT SITUATION IS A CHANCE TO PRACTICE WINNING

The position each of us takes—internally—will always determine how we react, how we respond to any occurrence that confronts us. If being stalled in traffic sends your blood pressure off the chart, wouldn't it seem smart to put yourself back in control?

If, in the past, aggravations have become hindrances, you can stop them from continuing to get in your way. If you have allowed the "details of life," the natural occurrences of daily living, to affect you negatively, upset you, get you off track, or ruin your day, you can change that, starting anytime you like.

If each of us at the moment of birth were given a quart jar of energy, and if we could use it up any way we chose, do you suppose most of us would use our energy in a wholesome, worthwhile way? I'm sure we'd like to. If you could choose for yourself, right now, how you were going to use the energy you have left, how would you use it? Would you scatter it about on anger, complaints, and the minor dissatisfactions of life? Or if you had only a limited amount, would you use it carefully, applying it to the thoughts and the tasks that would give you fulfillment and peace of mind?

The day each of us was born, we were given that energy—minute bits of electrochemical energy that feed small but important messages to our minds. One day, when the energy jar is empty, those thoughts, combined, will have created in our lives the sum total of every worthwhile thing we have done. Our thoughts are the gold coins in the treasure chest of our inheritance. Each one valuable by itself, they are the thoughts we are given to use any way we choose. When we recognize the incredible importance of every one of those small, energizing thoughts, why would we want to carelessly throw them away, use them up, without extracting the most we can get from each of them?

The next time a problem of any kind occurs, take note of how you respond to it. If you consider yourself to be a mature, capable individual, in control of yourself, *take control* of your thoughts. Not just when it suits you, and not just when things go well. Don't waste the power of your mind giving in to the petty inconveniences of life. Use that energy for something good. Channel it, control it, focus it. Give yourself the words and directions that put you in control of yourself. It isn't difficult, and it's always worth it.

CHAPTER TWENTY-TWO

Taking the First Steps

Following the steps of *Monitor, Edit,* and *Listen* that we discussed in chapter fifteen, pay attention to every word of self-talk that you say to yourself for the next several days. Bad, good, or otherwise, be aware of every word you say out loud or silently to yourself or about yourself. *Consciously* focus on everything you're thinking.

Pay attention to both kinds of self-talk—negative and positive. Notice especially the self-talk that creeps up unconsciously. If tomorrow morning the toast is burned, what will you say to yourself about it? If you've been thinking about doing something, but haven't yet gotten it done, bring the subject up. See what response you get from the *inside* you.

Notice the way you respond to problems and the way you react to opportunities. Watch your reaction to "risks." Is your old self-talk keeping you in the shadows or are you standing up and taking the right action? Does your self-talk say you are on top, confident, and going for it, or does it hold you back? Can you count yourself as being basically negative or basically positive? And most important of all—and be honest about this—have you been a negative self-talker or a positive self-talker?

As you're getting started, there is something else you can do to help you recognize, more clearly, your own programming and the role it's playing in your life. During the same time you're focusing on paying attention to your own self-talk, also notice the self-talk of the people around you, especially the people you spend your time with most. Pay attention to the self-talk of your own family members, your close friends, and the people you work with. Notice everything these people say in reference to themselves, and also what they think and feel about anything they talk about. And make special note of any negative self-talk you hear. There is no faster way to convince yourself how anti-productive negative self-talk can be than watching what happens to other people who do it.

For now, don't say anything to other people about their self-talk—just observe it. And while you're observing, also listen especially for what we call "opinions." Opinions reflect either our own beliefs or, when we have no opinion of our own, the beliefs of others. (All opinions are programs.) Observe what other people's self-talk reveals about their opinions, their beliefs, and their attitudes.

And, of course, the main reason to observe the self-talk of the people you spend your time with most is that those people are also wiring *your* brain with *their* programs. Without even knowing it, we can be wired with the programs of others—which is why we end up becoming most like the people we spend our time with most. (Which immediately suggests we should choose our friends very carefully.)

ANOTHER PRIMARY SOURCE OF PROGRAMMING

When you're starting to practice changing your self-talk by monitoring your own words and thoughts, and becoming aware of the programming of people around you, there is another source that is also wiring programs into your brain, and it is one you should be aware of and pay attention to. This major source of programs you're receiving each day is the "media"—the programming you get from television, newspapers, the Internet, et cetera.

The important thing to be aware of is how much programming you're getting from the media, and how you respond to the messages you're receiving. (Have you ever bought the brand of tissue you saw advertised the most often on television, or voted for a political candidate because of media presence?) Keep in mind that the secret to programming the brain is *repetition,* and that the part of the brain that stores all of our programs doesn't know the difference between something that's true, and something that's false. (Which can make television and the Internet very scary things.)

PUTTING YOURSELF IN CONTROL

The more aware you become of all of the persuasions and conditioning that go on in your life, the easier it will be for you to recognize them for what they are and know which of them to avoid and which to seek out. It's a healthy idea to stop every so often and ask yourself the question, "Who's in control here?" When you become aware of how programming works and where it comes from, who do you suppose is responsible for what gets programmed into your own mind? Once you're aware of it, *you* are, of course.

To some people, that could be a tough responsibility. But think how freeing it could be. Creating the thoughts that determine the direction of your own future is the most important personal responsibility you'll ever have—and accepting that responsibility can give you more control over your own life.

When you're aware of the programs you receive from yourself, from other people, from the media, and from the rest of the world around you, it's only natural that in the future, you would do everything possible to choose for yourself what that programming is, and where it comes from.

MAKE A "TOP TEN" LIST OF THE SELF-TALK YOU WANT TO CHANGE

To become consciously aware of your own self-talk now, write down the ten most significant negative self-talk suggestions you give yourself most often. Don't hedge, and don't mind being personal. List the negative self-talk phrases you use most. If you can't think of ten of them, keep trying. Most of us use dozens of self-talk phrases we're not even aware of until we start thinking about them.

Remember, these are negative self-talk phrases—things like "I can't . . ." "Nothing seems to go right," or "It's just not my day." What are the negative self-talk phrases that you use most often?

After you've thought of some of the negative things you say when you talk to yourself, or talk *about* yourself, it's easy to turn those phrases around. Any negative self-talk phrase you use can be turned into positive self-talk. In a short time you'll find that using self-talk the new way is just as easy and will come just as naturally to you as using it the old way.

Here are just a few examples of the kind of self-talk phrases we would find on a typical list of negative self-talk.

Example One:

The statement "**Things aren't going very well for me at work**" can easily be changed to "I enjoy my work. I understand the problems, I can deal with them, and I get past them."

Example Two:

Programming your subconscious with the self-defeating words "**I just can't seem to communicate with my son anymore**" can just as easily be rephrased into a new program: "I take the time to listen, talk, and communicate with my son. I'm patient and understanding. It's worth working at, and I do."

Example Three:

Telling yourself that you "**have a hard time getting out of bed in the morning**" certainly won't help you get out of bed any faster or easier. Every time the thought comes up, change the words to "It's easy for me to get out of bed in the morning. I like getting up and going for it." Repeat that to yourself for a few days—or for as long as it takes. Eventually you'll override the old program that made it tough for you to get up in the first place.

Keep in mind that changing just one or two phrases isn't going to make a sweeping change in your life. If you want to make some changes, change as many of the old phrases as you can find. The more of your old self-talk you change, and the more often you use the new self-talk when you talk to yourself about the subject, the better you'll do at making the change and making it permanent.

Example Four:

Instead of ever again telling yourself "**Today has been a tough day,**" think about what that tells your subconscious. If you are telling yourself that just because it was a difficult day it must have been a bad day, it can only make you feel less than successful that day. And all that does is convince your subconscious mind that you have failed.

Repeating anything that implies to your subconscious that you have failed will only convince it that failing is a pattern it should create. You don't have to pretend that the day was wonderful, but it isn't necessary to convince yourself that the day was a disaster, either. You worked hard and not everything worked out the way you wanted it to. Give yourself a break. Reshape the thought: *Today was fine. I feel good about myself. And tomorrow will be even better*. That's not ignoring the problems or the hard work. It's simply putting you back on top.

Example Five:

If you would really like to get yourself in better physical shape, but haven't gotten around to doing something about it, telling yourself "**I really need to get more exercise**" will only help you put it off. I like the self-talk phrase "I exercise every day." I would add a few supporting words like "I enjoy exercising and I really like how it makes me feel. I like keeping myself in shape mentally and physically. I look good and I feel good; and daily exercise keeps me that way. I look forward each day to exercising my body, exercising my mind, and keeping myself fit and winning."

Example Six:

"**I'd like to put more money into savings, but I just don't seem to be able to**" is the kind of money self-talk that many of us have used. Using it doesn't help a bit; it does just the opposite—it creates financial insecurity. We can just as easily wire our brains to create financially security: "I am good at earning what I need, and more. I'm good at saving money. Every month, without fail, I put something aside. Each week, each month, and each year, I do what I need to do to become financially more secure." Give your mind the right direction, the right challenge, and it will work just as hard to make things work for you as it has worked to hold you back.

Your subconscious mind has not found it difficult to make things tight financially—it just did what it had learned to do. If you don't make the change, neither will it. If you want to build a better financial base, have a talk with your subconscious. Tell it to do what you want it to do. And keep telling it. That will lead to a plan to do it, and the plan will lead to taking action. The results may not come overnight, but they will come.

Example Seven:

Change the words "**I wish I had more time**" to the words "I make time and I take time to do what I need to do." Almost no one has no time to spare. Even the busiest people can find the time they need to do what they truly choose to do; the problem usually comes up when we forget that we have some choice in how we spend our time. If not having enough time is a problem, I would also add: "I am responsible for choosing when, where, and how I spend my time. And I choose to spend my time in a way that creates the greatest benefits in my life."

As you get started, follow those examples of turning your words around, and practice doing that every day. The more you practice, the more naturally you'll begin to rewire the new kind of self-talk into your brain.

CHAPTER TWENTY-THREE

Overcoming Personal Growth Stasis

There is a challenge to becoming a true, positive self-talker and moving decisively forward, focusing every day on improving your self-talk and creating your exciting future. It is a challenge that is so important that I'm going to do my best to help you overcome it. It's called "PGS," or *personal growth stasis*.

Stasis, in personal growth, is the challenge that occurs when you stay in one place, and live between two opposing positions. In this case, the two opposing positions are 1) Where you've been up to now, and 2) Your unlimited future and where you'd like your life to go next. It happens when you're standing in the middle between your past and your future, not wanting to stay where you are, but not able to put yourself into action and launch forward with enough enthusiasm and belief to get you moving.

In the world of personal growth, stasis is the ultimate enemy. It means that no matter how great your enthusiasm for moving forward is at this moment, some of your past programs are working to hold you back—they want you to do nothing more than stay where you are. You want to move forward, but you're having trouble launching because the *old* programs that hold you back are *stronger* than your new goal to move forward. The result is, instead of moving wonderfully forward in your life, you end up staying where you are.

Living with the status quo, and failing to take the necessary steps to get better, is not something that only a few people face, and only now and then—it happens to almost everyone, and it happens a lot. (If you could rid the world of personal growth stasis for just one month, it would suddenly be a different world.)

So here you are, really wanting to make a change, fix the problem, or reach the goal, but your new awareness of self-talk, and how it feels to practice it, is not yet wired in.

Remember when we talked about the people who attended the pep rally and got motivated to change their lives, and then went home and did nothing about it? They failed to make the changes they so badly wanted to make because of stasis. As I pointed out in that chapter, all external motivation is temporary; they couldn't take the moment home with them, so stasis won.

WHAT PERSONAL GROWTH STASIS ACTUALLY DOES

PGS doesn't just stop you. It harms you in ways you're not even aware of. Here are just a few examples of what it actually does.

Personal growth stasis:

- Stops your growth
- Wastes your time
- Drains your energy
- Lowers your self-esteem
- Affects your health
- Makes you feel guilty

- Keeps you off focus
- Justifies doing nothing
- Stops you from setting new goals
- Makes inaction a habit
- Reinforces negative programs
- Causes you to fail

Part of the problem is that living with stasis is incredibly energy-draining and gets you nowhere while it constantly chips away at your self-esteem. (How can you possibly feel good about yourself if you don't believe you're doing what you should be doing?)

But perhaps the biggest problem of all is that living in stasis robs you of your spirit, the wonderful, greater part of you that sees the better you, and whose job it is to take you to your greatest heights. When we lose that spirit, or ignore its call to action, we not only lose a part of ourselves, we also lose ascending to the level of who we were born to be in the first place.

SEEING THE FACES OF POSSIBILITY

I have often stood in front of audiences, talking about the breakthrough of self-talk, and how each of us can put it to work in our lives—and while speaking, I've watched the faces of the people in front of me. During my talk or seminar, I have gone into step-by-step detail on how the brain gets programmed, and in even more detail on what each of us can do to take our lives back.

Speaking not as a motivator but as someone bringing a message of deliverance, I watch the people in the audience as one by one they "get it," an expression of new hope comes over them, and they realize that they are about to be released from the invisible shackles that have bound them. You can see it in their faces.

But I know that the moment they leave and return to their homes, I cannot motivate them to do anything at all. While they sit in front of me, I watch their faces, and I see their spirits rise and their potential come to life. But when I see this, I have to work to keep my own heart from falling, because I know from speaking to these wonderful people for thirty years of my life that out of the hundreds or thousands of those who are seated in front of me now, only a handful of them will do anything at all with the new gift of truth I have just presented to them.

So many speakers, trainers, and teachers have felt what I feel then. We know our goal is to help others change their lives for the better. We know we have some of the answers that will help. And we despair that only a few of them will do it. (We also fear that those who need it most will do the least, even though it could mean so much.)

Looking across those audiences, I see the parents who want to bring their newborn baby up without the negative programs that will try to diminish her life. I see the older couple who now recognize that they may have missed a lot, but there is still time left. I see the businesspeople who realize they can finally set and reach the goals they had only dreamed of. I see the teenage girl who grasps the ideas of self-talk clearly, and decides to make her own words an example of positive self-talk that she will use for the rest of her life. I see the nurse, the parent, the office worker, the teacher, the network marketer, the waitress, the manager, and the student. And each of them understands, and I can see each of them vowing to themselves to take a stand, seize the future, and make it their own.

Having worked in this field for much of my life, I know that every one of those people could reach nearly unlimited heights of personal growth and change if the message of self-talk stayed vibrantly alive within them after the seminar was over. But motivation doesn't last, and even the strongest of dreams fades quickly in the morning light.

GETTING PAST STASIS

But I have also learned that if you want to avoid stasis—and I hope that you will—you can. There are some things you can do.

Since you have gotten to this point in the book, I can almost imagine you sitting in front of me, like someone in one of those audiences. We have come quite a ways together, and I have done my best to share my message with you in a way that is understandable, with steps forward that are clear and easy to follow. If I could see your face right now, I can imagine seeing someone of great potential, someone who "gets it," understands the message, and is ready to move forward.

I would then tell you, as your mentor would, speaking to you from the heart, the most encouraging words I could ever say: "I believe in you. You can do this, and you know you can."

Here then, are those things I would tell you to do to get past stasis.

1. As you read this, set a goal to bring positive self-talk permanently into your life.

Right now, pause and think about it for a moment. Set a goal. If you can, write it down. A goal that is not written down has a less than 10 percent chance of coming to life. The moment you write the same goal down on paper, the chances of your achieving that goal immediately climb to 75 percent or more.

Use your own words if you choose, but write the goal something like this: My goal is *to practice positive self-talk every day, and make it a permanent part of my life.*

Then read that goal every morning and every night just before you go to sleep for the next ninety days.

2. Listen to self-talk sessions a minimum of fifteen minutes a day.

At the time of this writing, there is a special website* that allows you to listen to self-talk sessions for thirty days at no charge, so listening won't cost you anything.

Listening to daily sessions of repeated self-talk phrases will help you begin to wire in the language of self-talk, and it will also override the stasis and get you started. The self-talk sessions you'll listen to cover a broad variety of topics. They are streamed directly to your phone or your tablet, and they work best if you just let them play in the background while you're going about your day.

While the purpose of listening to self-talk sessions is to rewire your brain with positive programs for the long term, listening each day will also give you the inspiration to stay with it long enough for the new programs to begin to be wired in.

Although I hesitate to sound in any way commercial in recommending that you listen to self-talk sessions that I wrote and produced, if we were talking together right now, and I were your coach or mentor, that is exactly what I would recommend that you do.

---

* For a link to the website to listen to self-talk sessions, go to www.shadhelmstetter.com.

3. Write a list of the old negative self-talk programs you've been using in the past that you'd like to change.

Just as in writing out your goals, this will also work best if you actually write your list down on paper. Think of any negative self-talk that you have used more than once, or that you use often, and write it down. (If you wrote out a "Top Ten" list as recommended in the previous chapter, you can begin with that list.)

The reason for doing this is that when you want to overcome stasis, it's all about *awareness* and *focus*. The more you're aware of your self-talk and your goal to change it each day, the more you focus on doing that, the more neural activity you'll create, and the faster and stronger you'll begin to wire the new directions into your brain.

If you follow those recommendations, you will be able to defeat stasis. You'll become a positive self-talker, and your life will change in wonderful ways. And all those dreams you've dreamed will have the chance to come true.

Let me repeat, *You can do this, and I know you can.*

CHAPTER TWENTY-FOUR

To Change or Not to Change

At this moment, or at some time in the future, you may be making the decision to make a change. Let me give you a few words of encouragement. It is likely that you already know what you would like to do. If that is the case, if your innermost mind tells you that it is time, then it is time.

When Shakespeare wrote the words "To be, or not to be . . . ," he may not have known that he touched the essence of *self.* To *be,* or not to *be,* that *is* the question. To become or not to become; to achieve or not to achieve; to *do* or not to do—the answer to that question is the answer that will determine the future—and the success—of each of us.

It's a good idea to take stock of our progress. It's healthy to ask ourselves how well we are doing. We have the right and the need to gauge, judge, and assess our own forward motion. *Are we getting anywhere or aren't we? Are we getting by or are we doing the best that we can? Are we doing what we want to do or would we like to do something else, something better?* Do we have every part of ourselves in line and in tune with our finest expectations, or would we like to make a change or two?

Most of us have changes we would like to make in our lives. There are times when we want to make a small change, something that will help us do something differently, or deal with something in a better way than we dealt with it in the past. There are other times when we would like to make a sweeping change—out with the old and in with the new.

If making life "work" is as simple as making a few changes, why don't you do it?

WOULD YOU LIKE TO MAKE A CHANGE?

I have known people who wanted nothing more than to fix a problem at home or at work, or wanted to change some small thing about themselves or in their lives that would help them grow or make life a little easier. I have also known people who were fed up with everything. They wanted to change their lives in a major way—different job, new husband or wife, sell out and move to another state—they wanted to do whatever it would take to change their lives and change their futures. I have known people who tried to change their lives by changing their homes, cars, or careers.

But for most of them the *change* wasn't a real change; it didn't work. They took their old selves with them. Changes of heart are as fragile and as temporary as changes of costumes in a play. We can change friends, spouses, jobs, or locations, and we will still take the same inner selves along with us—the same internal identities that made us unhappy, helped us, or got us into trouble in the first place. If we take the old images of ourselves with us wherever we go and into whatever we do, how could we expect to do better the next time we try?

If we want to make any important change in our beliefs, attitudes, emotions, behavior, actions, or results, we should, at the outset, decide who is in command—and who or what is in control of the changes that take place.

How would you identify the changes that are happening in your life? Are they the result of accident, destiny, circumstance, or personal decision?

Change occurs either as a result of something outside of you that happens *to you,* or as a result of something within yourself that causes the change to take place.

CHANGE CREATED BY OUTSIDE INFLUENCES

With this external kind of change, there is no major psychological impact that alerts us to the fact that the change is happening. There is nothing traumatic about this kind of change—in fact there is nothing noticeable about it at all. This change happens normally and casually. It is the result of the relentless, unseen waves of external influence, day after day, hour by hour, shaping and reshaping the shorelines of our thinking. The kind of change that happens *to* us is the result of those minor attitude changes that come to us by way of expectations; minor events; company policies; personal relationships; relatives; family needs; parental authority; religious credos; peer pressures; advertising of all kinds; economic trends; daily exposure to television, radio, magazines, and newspapers; social requirements; political positions; whimsical notions; close friends; and offhand comments.

It is strange that these influences should shape most of our lives for us; and yet they do. They are not all bad or contrary, of course; some of them are necessary and worthwhile. Some of these influences—a few of them—are the best kind we can ever hope to find. But taken as a group, these everyday influences in our lives are seldom the notes on which great symphonies are played. More often they are dirges, plainly written tunes, written in the key of average, with a slowly meandering discordant melody, leading to something less than the rising crescendo of great finales we had hoped for, never once demanding or creating the lasting and beautiful orchestration of a life well lived.

The conditioning of daily living somehow convinces us that mankind's greatest need, *social survival,* is also each person's greatest achievement.

The result is that we slowly, unknowingly, change not to achieve—but to *survive,* in a way that offers us the acceptance of others. We get by. We do what we must. We do as well as we can, get along with others as well as possible, play our roles, do our jobs, put a little away for the future, and hope for the best. *The dreams we dreamed as children, we learn no longer to believe.*

That is the tune we are taught to play. Instead of believing, *knowing* that each of us is an entire orchestra, we are led to believe we are only the flute. We listen to the idle gossip of a friend, follow the lead of so-called leaders, fit our lives into a mold that was not of our making, tuck our dreams in our pockets, and hope for better things to come.

And so we are changed by the lives we live. For most of us it is seldom the calamitous change of catastrophic events. It is the slow, sure change of environment—the change forced upon us by the world around us. What we become a part *of* becomes a part of *us.* What we perceive and what we accept are important parts of what we, too, will become.

THE CHANGE THAT'S CREATED BY PERSONAL CHOICE

The one kind of change in our lives that is left up to the individual—to each of us—is the change that is created by personal *choice.*

Have you ever thought about the fact that what you do, how you live, what you become, is almost entirely up to you? Of course there are outside circumstances to deal with, but how you deal with them is still, and finally, up to no one else but you. *What you decide to do next will determine what you do next.*

Make the decision to do what you choose and your next step will be your own. Sit back and let the outside world take the lead, and it will. Decide to determine your own next step—and thereby your future—and you can. Make the decision to make each breath you breathe your own. Stick by it, and each breath, step, motion, and achievement will be of your own making and of your own choice.

The research of neuroscience has proved that what you determine for yourself, what you conceive and give your energies to, will create or call upon a life force that will turn the dreams you dream into touchable reality. But we have only recently learned the process that makes it work: *Learn how to think what you think and you will begin to determine and redirect most of your future for yourself.* If you learn *how* to think *what* you think, you will put yourself back in control.

Just as it is the thoughts, ideas, demands, and influences of others that have guided, controlled, and directed most of our lives in the past, it is the personal control of our own minds that now gives us the chance to change our futures—for ourselves.

You can do so much. You can, if you choose, break through the wall that stands between you and anything you would like to change or achieve. Give yourself the will to do it. Give yourself the belief, the attitude, the emotion, and the action that will get you where you want to be.

THE FINAL DIFFERENCE

We began this journey through the workings of the mind and through the maze of possible solutions with my own personal search for an answer that not only would work, but also would keep on working. Temporary success is fine, but something that turns temporary success into a permanent way of life makes a lot more sense. Living each day in a more successful way is what each of us, somewhere within us, would like to achieve.

In many ways, we have come far. We have achieved almost unimagined heights in our technology, in our material wealth. We have more conveniences, more tools, more appliances in life than the wealthiest of kings and queens had in their lives only a few decades ago. Through our medicine and our science, we have extended the potential for living more years on earth than was ever thought possible even a few generations in the past. We have conquered the shallow envelope of space that surrounds us. We have learned to manage our businesses, some of our environment, and a small part of our destiny.

And finally, with help from the field of neuroscience, we have learned to manage the one part of our lives that is the heart and substance of everything we will ever do. We have learned to manage our own minds.

THE SOLUTION

Learning to manage, control, and direct the resources of your own mind are the greatest opportunities you will ever have.

Until recently we didn't even know the name of our greatest adversary—that wall that has confined us to the smallest part of what we could have been. The adversary has been *us*. It is the thoughts that we have thought. It is our own thinking that has created the limited self-portraits of who we believed ourselves to be.

Our technology has given us the tools, and science has shown us the way. Our emerging understanding of our own human brain has pointed us in the right direction. We have learned that what we do, and what we do with *us,* is not an accidental happening. We have learned that *who* we are and *what* we are is the result of more than a chance combination of genetic inclinations. We have learned that what happens next—for each of us—is more up to us than we might have *thought:* It is up to us what we *think*.

Talk to yourself. Learn the words—the right words—*wire them in*, and use them. Make your self-talk a positive, everyday, self-directing habit. Talk to yourself in a way that is *kind, loving, caring, strong, demanding,* and *determined.* Talk to yourself in the right way, every day.

When you do, you will give yourself the greatest gift you will ever give. Remember,

You are everything that is,
your thoughts, your life, your dreams come true.
You are everything you choose to be.
You are as unlimited as the endless universe.

INFORMATION AND RESOURCES

Self-Talk Audio Programs
www.shadhelmstetter.com

Self-Talk Training
www.selftalkinstitute.com

Life-Coach Training
www.lifecoachinstitute.com